CREATING TRAUMA-I

OXFORD WORKSHOP SERIES:

SCHOOL SOCIAL WORK ASSOCIATION OF AMERICA

Series Advisory Board

Ethical Decision Making in School Mental Health
James C. Raines and Nic T. Dibble

Functional Behavioral Assessment:
A Three-Tiered Prevention Model
Kevin J. Filter and Michelle E. Alvarez

School Bullying:
New Perspectives on a Growing Problem
David R. Dupper

Consultation Theory and Practice:
A Handbook for School Social Workers
Christine Anlauf Sabatino

School-Based Practice with Children and Youth Experiencing Homelessness
James P. Canfield

Family Engagement with Schools:
Strategies for School Social Workers and Educators
Nancy Feyl Chavkin

Solution-Focused Brief Therapy in Schools
A 360-Degree View of the Research and Practice Principles, Second Edition
Johnny Kim, Michael Kelly, Cynthia Franklin

Evidence-Based Practice in School Mental Health:
Addressing DSM-5 Disorders in Schools, Second Edition
James C. Raines

Creating Trauma-Informed Schools:
A Guide for School Social Workers and Educators
Eileen A. Dombo and Christine Anlauf Sabatino

CREATING TRAUMA-INFORMED SCHOOLS

A Guide for School Social Workers and Educators

Eileen A. Dombo
and Christine Anlauf Sabatino

The National Catholic School of Social Service
The Catholic University of America

OXFORD WORKSHOP SERIES

OXFORD
UNIVERSITY PRESS

OXFORD
UNIVERSITY PRESS

Oxford University Press is a department of the University of Oxford. It furthers
the University's objective of excellence in research, scholarship, and education
by publishing worldwide. Oxford is a registered trade mark of Oxford University
Press in the UK and certain other countries.

Published in the United States of America by Oxford University Press
198 Madison Avenue, New York, NY 10016, United States of America.

Library of Congress Cataloging-in-Publication Data
Names: Dombo, Eileen A., author. | Sabatino, Christine Anlauf, author.
Title: Creating trauma-informed schools : a guide for school social workers
and educators / Eileen A. Dombo, Christine Anlauf Sabatino.
Description: New York, NY : Oxford University Press, [2019] |
Series: Oxford workshop series: School social work association of America |
Includes bibliographical references and index.
Identifiers: LCCN 2018041097 (print) | LCCN 2018055832 (ebook) |
ISBN 9780190873813 (updf) | ISBN 9780190873820 (epub) |
ISBN 9780190873837 (Online Component) | ISBN 9780190873806 (pbk. : alk. paper)
Subjects: LCSH: School social work—United States. | Psychic trauma in children—
United States. | Psychic trauma in adolescence—United States. |
Children with social disabilities—Education—United States. |
Teenagers with social disabilities—Education—United States.
Classification: LCC LB3013.4 (ebook) | LCC LB3013.4 .D66 2019 (print) |
DDC 371.7—dc23
LC record available at https://lccn.loc.gov/2018041097

3 5 7 9 8 6 4 2

Printed by Webcom, Inc., Canada

This book is dedicated to the school social workers, teachers, administrators, and staff who enter schools every day to teach our children and keep them safe.

Contents

Preface

Do you need help to create a trauma-informed school?

Do you need information to support students who experience stressful or dangerous events?

In this book, you will learn how to provide leadership in the delivery of trauma-informed services in a school setting. It will:

- discuss the impact of trauma on child and adolescent development and academic learning,
- identify the pillars needed to create a safe school environment,
- lay out 11 principles of trauma-informed services,
- offer an overview of empirically supported direct practice interventions grouped by developmental stages,
- explore frameworks for engaging teachers, families, and kids in creating trauma-informed school environments, and
- describe a program evaluation strategy for progress monitoring and determining the success of the services.

Each chapter contains tables, figures, text boxes, case examples, or online resources that supplement the information presented.

Ready to begin?

Acknowledgments

This book would not have been possible without support from three graduate students at The Catholic University of America's National Catholic School of Social Service. Our gratitude goes to Ksenia Dombo, Cara Morro, and Nicole Toscano for all their assistance. We feel blessed by the generosity of Jim Raines, PhD, President of the School Social Work Association of America and Professor of Social Work at California State University, Monterey Bay. His valuable contributions in Chapters 2, 3, and 4 with text boxes on resilience, epigenetics, and school safety and gun violence add a great deal to the book. For giving us the perspective of current school social workers and adding some case context, we give thanks to Carol Sabatino and Maggie Wilkerson.

CREATING TRAUMA-INFORMED SCHOOLS

I

Introduction

Today students are exposed to direct and indirect forms of trauma borne of socioeconomic and political discord, creating the need for the school community to address the mental health needs of children and adolescents to promote successful school experiences. Children at all educational levels, from Early Head Start settings through high school, are vulnerable to abuse, neglect, bullying, violence in their homes and neighborhoods, and other traumatic life events. Research shows that upward of 70% of children in schools report experiencing at least one traumatic event before age 16 (Layne et al., 2011).

Schools must tackle situations in which trauma plays a key role in micro, mezzo, and macro educational disruptions. Students struggle to regulate their emotions, producing obstacles to their learning capacities. Difficulty modulating internalizing and externalizing behaviors fosters additional issues in school on top of preexisting traumatic experiences. Classrooms and learning groups are unable to stay on task. Students who act out disrupt schoolrooms and study groups, interfering with the teaching-learning experience for educators and students. School communities see trauma-driven difficulties translated into home-school-community problems. Graduation rates, expulsion, discipline issues, and poor academic scores tax available resources in the school and community. The correlation between high rates of trauma exposure and poor academic performance is established in the scholarly literature (Perfect et al., 2016), as is the need for trauma-informed schools and communities (Walkley & Cox, 2013).

The Role of the School Social Worker

The basic assumption of this book is that school social workers are in a position to provide leadership, knowledge, and skills to create trauma-informed schools and foster resilience in schoolchildren. Since its inception, the role of the school social worker has been to be attuned to societal conditions that adversely affect the lives of children and "aid in the reorganization of school administration practices by supplying evidence of unfavorable conditions that underlie pupils' school difficulties and pointing out needed changes" (Allen-Meares, 2015, p. 7). Applying the contemporary ecological perspective, general systems theory, and theories of human behavior, school social workers are able to give voice to the complex interrelated factors associated with trauma and its impact on childhood development and educational advancement within the school context. Trauma-informed schools aim to address students' dysfunctional academic and behavioral performance driven by affective and physiological arousal. Furthermore, our distinct professional approach that examines the transactions between persons and their environments, a holistic analysis, uniquely positions school social workers to ask appropriate questions, collaborate with decision-makers, treat traumatic stress in children and adolescents, balance organizational/administrative needs with student needs, and monitor progress in implementing change to create safe spaces for traumatized students to grow and learn.

Plan for the Book

There are scant resources for social workers to assist in the creation of trauma-informed schools. This book will provide an overview of the impact of trauma on children and adolescents, as well as interventions for direct practice and collaboration with teachers, families, and communities. Readers will discover distinct examples of how to implement the ten principles of trauma-informed services in their schools and how to provide trauma-informed care to students that are grounded in the principles of safety, connection, and emotional regulation. They will also gain beneficial skills for self-care in their work.

Chapter 2 outlines the most current research on trauma. Data from the Adverse Childhood Experiences Study (ACES) (Anda et al., 2006), as well as other academic and epidemiological studies, is used to address the negative impact of traumatic experiences on child development. The neurobiology of trauma is explored along with other psychosocial effects of abuse, neglect, and other adverse experiences affecting children in the United States.

Research shows that children and adolescents who experience abuse and neglect have lower learning outcomes, higher rates of learning difficulties, and higher rates of mental health disorders and behavioral challenges than children without these traumatic experiences (Holmes et al., 2015; Layne et al., 2011; Mendelson et al., 2015; Perfect et al., 2016). Chapter 3 explores some of the common social, emotional, behavioral, and academic issues seen in children who experience trauma. Information to help school social workers with the process of differential diagnosis and differentiation among symptoms of posttraumatic stress disorder, attention deficit hyperactivity disorder, and the cognitive and intellectual issues that require special education is provided.

Chapter 4 takes an in-depth look at the three pillars of trauma-informed care in schools: safety, connection, and managing emotions. These three pillars are foundations that must be present in any setting because they are crucial elements on which trauma-informed environments are built (van der Kolk & Courtois, 2005). Examples of how to create a school environment with these core components are provided.

The ten principles of trauma-informed services are applied to school environments in Chapter 5. Each of the ten principles (Elliott et al., 2005) is explored in depth with examples of how to apply each in a school setting. An 11th principle, care of the worker, is added to address vicarious trauma (VT). Resources and supports for ameliorating the effects of VT on workforce health are also provided.

Direct practice with kids who experience abuse, neglect, and other forms of trauma is discussed in Chapter 6. The chapter offers readers an overview of the current, evidence-supported interventions for use in direct practice with children and adolescents in school settings. It is divided by developmental stages to provide appropriate strategies for preschool, elementary, middle, and high school students. Examples of the interventions are the Attachment, Self-Regulation, and Competency (ARC) model; Cognitive Behavioral Intervention for Trauma in Schools (CBITS); Trauma-Focused Cognitive Behavioral Therapy (TF-CBT); and Structured Psychotherapy for Adolescents Responding to Chronic Stress (SPARCS) (Holmes et al., 2015; Mendelson et al., 2015). Case examples are provided to demonstrate how these interventions are used in practice.

Chapter 7 explores the essential framework for engaging teachers, families, and students in creating trauma-informed school environments. The framework creates a customized model for schools that engage all stakeholders in this paradigm shift. Models of trauma-informed schools are reviewed, as well as lessons learned from other areas of social work practice, such as child welfare and mental health (Ko et al., 2008).

This final chapter discusses evaluation strategies for trauma-informed school social workers to utilize in determining the success of their programs and to adapt programs as needed based on process and outcome research. Resources for contributing to the body of knowledge in this area are also provided to assist school social workers in publishing scholarly manuscripts on their findings.

The correlation between high rates of trauma exposure and poor academic performance is established in the scholarly literature (Perfect et al., 2016), as is the need for trauma-informed schools and communities (Walkley & Cox, 2013). However, researchers are now finding negative effects on school outcomes for children who have not directly experienced trauma but whose classmates have (Burdick-Will, 2018). This means that *all* children benefit from trauma-informed schools. School social workers are on the front lines of service delivery through their work with children who face social and emotional struggles in the pursuit of education (Ko et al., 2008). We are in a prime position to prevent and address trauma, and this book provides current knowledge and concrete skills to guide development of trauma-informed schools, helping students succeed in school.

Resources

National Child Traumatic Stress Network (NCTSN)

1. National Child Traumatic Stress Network Schools Committee. (2008). *Child trauma toolkit for educators.* Los Angeles, CA & Durham, NC: National Center for Child Traumatic Stress. Retrieved from http://www.nctsn.org/sites/default/files/assets/pdfs/Child_Trauma_Toolkit_Final.pdf

   The "Child Trauma Toolkit for Educators" guide created by the NCTSN presents a comprehensive overview of the prevalence of trauma exposure in children and adolescents and how exposure to trauma can affect school performance and interfere with learning. The guide provides suggestions for educators and school personnel on how to help children who are experiencing symptoms related to trauma.

2. National Child Traumatic Stress Network. (2018). *Psychological first aid for schools (PFA-S)*. Los Angeles, CA & Durham, NC: National Center for Child Traumatic Stress. Retrieved from http://www.nctsn.org/content/psychological-first-aid-schoolspfa

   The Psychological First Aid for Schools (PFA-S) webpage outlines an evidence-informed approach to assisting adults, adolescents, children, and families after a traumatic event. The core actions of the approach focus on safety, stabilization, practical assistance, connection, and linkage to community resources. This manual includes additional resources for school personnel working with children and adolescents in a school setting.

3. National Child Traumatic Stress Network Schools Committee. (2013). *Back to school resources for school personnel*. Los Angeles, CA & Durham, NC: National Center for Child Traumatic Stress. Retrieved from http://www.nctsn.org/sites/default/files/assets/pdfs/school_resource_list_final.pdf

   The "Back to School Resources for School Personnel" resource list provides an overview of issues related to trauma and how trauma can affect children and adolescents, as well as tools to help support students and families affected by trauma. The resources include fact sheets, tips, interventions, and webinars that are free and available to download in both English and Spanish.

Substance Abuse and Mental Health Services Administration (SAMHSA)

1. National Child Traumatic Stress Initiative. (2015). *Understanding child trauma*. Rockville, MD: Substance Abuse and Mental Health Services Administration. Retrieved from https://www.samhsa.gov/sites/default/files/programs_campaigns/nctsi/nctsi-infographic-full.pdf

   This infographic provides facts highlighting the prevalence and pervasiveness of childhood trauma, as well as common signs of traumatic stress in young children, elementary school–aged children, and adolescents. The infographic also provides tips for working with children and adolescents exposed to trauma and highlights the importance of supportive caregiving systems on the recovery process.

2. Substance Abuse and Mental Health Services Administration. (2017). *Coping with traumatic events: Resources for children, parents, educators, and other professionals*. Retrieved from https://www.samhsa.gov/capt/tools-learning-resources/coping-traumatic-events-resources

   This webpage on SAMHSA's website provides a list of publications and resources that provide tips and suggestions on a variety of issues related to the impact of trauma on children and adolescents. Resources are categorized by age group and type of trauma.

3. Substance Abuse and Mental Health Services Administration. (2016). *SAMHSA's efforts to address trauma and violence*. Retrieved from https://www.samhsa.gov/topics/trauma-violence/samhsas-trauma-informed-approach

   This webpage on SAMHSA's website highlights key principles for delivering trauma-informed services and creating trauma-informed settings. This webpage provides suggestions for providing trauma-informed services to address various traumatic incidents, such as school violence, bullying, and natural disasters.

National Institute of Mental Health (NIMH)

1. National Institute of Mental Health. (2017). *Coping with traumatic events.* Bethesda, MD: National Institute of Mental Health. Retrieved from https://www.nimh.nih.gov/health/topics/coping-with-traumatic-events/index.shtml

   The "Coping with Traumatic Events" webpage provides examples of emotional and physical signs of trauma following a traumatic event. This webpage also provides free handouts and brochures on how to help children and adolescents cope after traumatic events.

2. National Institute of Mental Health. (2015). *Helping children and adolescents cope with violence and disasters: For teachers, clergy, and other adults in the community.* Bethesda, MD: National Institute of Mental Health. Retrieved from https://www.nimh.nih.gov/health/publications/helping-children-and-adolescents-cope-with-violence-and-disasters-community-members/helpingchildren-communitymembers-508_150143.pdf

   This brochure by NIMH defines trauma and provides an overview of common emotional and behavioral responses to trauma, categorized by age group. The brochure also provides comprehensive steps that adults, such as school personnel or other community members, can take to target specific emotional or behavioral trauma responses in children or adolescents.

US Department of Education

1. U.S. Department of Education. (2005). *Tips for helping students recovering from traumatic events.* Washington, DC: U.S. Department of Education. Retrieved from https://www2.ed.gov/parents/academic/help/recovering/recovering.pdf

   This brochure provides practical information for working with and helping students of all ages after a traumatic incident. The target audience includes parents, teachers, school counselors and social workers, coaches, and administrators. Although this brochure focuses on natural disasters, the tips provided could be applied to a variety of other traumas that students may experience.

American Psychological Association (APA)

1. American Psychological Association Presidential Task Force on Posttraumatic Stress Disorder and Trauma in Children and Adolescents. (2008). *Children and trauma: Update for mental health professionals.* Washington, DC: American Psychological Association. Retrieved from http://www.apa.org/pi/families/resources/update.pdf

   This brochure provides an overview of what we already know about the impact of trauma on children and adolescents and highlights what mental health professionals across settings, including schools, can do to help children and adolescents who are exposed to trauma.

National Association for Social Workers (NASW) Press

1. Varianides, A. (2016). *The school social work toolkit.* Washington, DC: National Association for Social Workers (NASW) Press. Retrieved from https://www.naswpress.org/publications/clinical/school-social-work-toolkit.html

The NASW Press has created a toolkit for school social workers that serves as a "how-to" guide for mental health professionals in education. The toolkit provides concrete activities for working with youths, group activities, workshop resources, tips on communication with parents, and crisis intervention assessment and protocols.

Oxford University Press

1. Anderson-Ketchmark, C., & Alvarez, M. E. (2009). Addressing trauma in schools: An online resource. *Children & Schools*, *31*(3), 189–191. Retrieved from https://academic. oup.com/cs/article-abstract/31/3/189/351587?redirectedFrom=fulltext
This article serves as a resource for mental health professionals in education working with youths who have experienced trauma. Topics include communication, skills, attentiveness, handling emotions, impulsiveness, anger, withdrawal, and relationships with peers and school personnel.

Related Resources

Helping Children Cope with the Challenges of War and Terrorism. Retrieved from http://www.7-dippity.com/other/op_hcc.html
This workbook provides activities for parents and children about how to help cope with feelings and thoughts related to war and possible threats of terrorists attacks. This workbook also includes a supplemental book for school personnel about how to adapt these activities to the school setting.

National Alliance for Grieving Children. (2017). *Home*. Retrieved from https://childrengrieve.org/
This website provides useful resources about how to talk to children and adolescents about and cope with grief and loss. The content addresses various types of loss and can be adapted to the school setting.

The Dougy Center: The National Center for Grieving Children and Families. (2018). *When death impacts your school*. Retrieved from https://www.dougy.org/grief-resources/death-impacts-your-school/
This article by The Dougy Center: The National Center for Grieving Children and Families provides suggestions for teachers and school administrators about how to communicate with youths about grief and loss, as well as do's and don'ts when it comes to communicating and working with grieving children.

The National Institute for Trauma and Loss in Children. (2018). *Trauma resources*. Retrieved from https://www.starr.org/tlc/childhood_trauma
The National Institute for Trauma and Loss in Children website provides extensive research and resources for parents and professionals about childhood trauma, as well as tools for working with children who have been exposed to trauma.

References

Allen-Meares, P. (2015). Social work services in schools (7th ed.). New York, NY: Pearson Education.

Anda, R. F., Felitti, V. J., Bremner, J. D., Walker, J. D., Whitfield, C., Perry, B. D., Dube, S. R., & Giles, W. H. (2006). The enduring effects of abuse and related adverse experiences in childhood: A convergence of evidence from neurobiology and epidemiology. *European Archives of Psychiatry and Clinical Neuroscience, 256*(3), 174–186.

Burdick-Will, J. (2018). Neighborhood violence, peer effects, and academic achievement in Chicago. *Sociology of Education, 91*(3), 205–223.

Elliot, D., Bjelajac, P., Fallot, R., Markoff, L., & Reed, B. (2005). Trauma-informed or trauma-denied: Principles and implementation of trauma-informed services for women. *Journal of Community Psychology, 33*(4), 461–477.

Holmes, C., Levy, M., Smith, A., Pinne, S., & Neese, P. (2015). A model for creating a supportive trauma-informed culture for children in preschool settings. *Journal of Child and Family Studies, 24,* 1650–1659.

Ko, S. J., Ford, J. D., Kassam-Adams, N., Berkowitz, S. J., Wilson, C., Wong, M., Brymer, M. J., & Layne, C. M. (2008). Creating trauma-informed systems: Child welfare, education, first responders, health care, and juvenile justice. *Professional Psychology: Research and Practice, 39*(4), 396–404.

Layne, C. M., Ippen, C. G., Strand, V., Stuber, M., Abramovitz, R., Reyes, G., Jackson, L. A., Ross, L., Curtis, A., Lipscomb, A., & Pynoos, R. (2011). The Core Curriculum on Childhood Trauma: A tool for training a trauma-informed workforce. *Psychological Trauma: Theory, Research, Practice, and Policy, 3*(3), 243–252.

Mendelson, T., Tandon, S. D., O'Brennan, L., Leaf, P. J., & Ialongo, N. S. (2015). Brief report: Moving prevention into schools: The impact of a trauma-informed school-based intervention. *Journal of Adolescence, 43,* 142–147.

Perfect, M. M., Turley, M. R., Carlson, J. S., Yohanna, J., & Gilles, M. P. S. (2016). School-related outcomes of traumatic event exposure and traumatic stress symptoms in students: A systematic review of research from 1990 to 2015. *School Mental Health, 8*(1), 7–43.

van der Kolk, B., & Courtois, C. (2005). Editorial comments: Complex developmental trauma. *Journal of Traumatic Stress, 18*(5), 385–388.

Walkley, M., & Cox, T. L. (2013). Building trauma-informed schools and communities. *Children & Schools, 35*(2), 123–126.

2

███

Trauma and Its Sequelae in Children and Adolescents

The most current research on trauma and child development demonstrates that there are significant risk factors for school success. At the same time, resilience and protective factors help other children overcome these obstacles. This chapter will explore the effects of trauma on children and adolescents. Data from the Adverse Childhood Experiences Study, as well as other academic and epidemiological studies, will be used to address the negative impact of traumatic experiences on child development. The neurobiology of trauma will also be explored along with other psychosocial effects of abuse, neglect, and other adverse experiences affecting children in the United States.

Adverse Experiences in Childhood and Adolescence

The Centers for Disease Control and Prevention (CDC) and Kaiser Permanente studied whether negative childhood experiences affect a person's health and well-being throughout their life (US Department of Health and Human Services, National Center for Injury Prevention and Control, Division of Violence Prevention, 2016). The study examined more than 17,000 children in Southern California using physical exams and surveys concerning childhood experiences, current health status, and behaviors. The study found the following ten adverse childhood experiences (ACEs) that pose strong risk factors for decreased health and overall well-being throughout a person's life:

Types of Adverse Childhood Experiences
1. Emotional abuse
2. Emotional neglect
3. Physical abuse
4. Physical neglect

5. Sexual abuse
6. Mother treated violently
7. Substance abuse in the home
8. Mental illness of household member
9. Separation/divorce of parents
10. Incarceration of household member

Participants in the study were from the general population, with strong generalizability of the findings. The findings indicated that two-thirds of participants lived through at least one ACE, and 25% reported the presence of three or more ACEs. The ACEs and negative outcomes have a *graded dose-response relationship*, meaning that as the number and intensity of the ACEs increased, so did the negative outcomes. In other words, the higher the number of adverse experiences, the higher the chance for disrupted neurological development; impaired social, emotional, and cognitive functioning; risky health behaviors; poorer health outcomes; and early death. For the school-aged child, these ten experiences can have profound impacts on their ability to function successfully in a traditional school setting. In addition to the ten ACE categories, children can be exposed to the trauma experienced by parents while still developing in utero (Sandman, Davis, Buss, & Glynn, 2012) and outside their home during childhood. Other types of traumatic experiences not addressed in the Adverse Childhood Experiences Study include traumatic loss, medical trauma, natural disasters, immigration and refugee experiences, terrorism, human trafficking, and community violence.

Impact of Trauma

The effects of exposure to traumatic events vary for each individual. A traumatic experience can be temporarily distressing or can have longer-lasting, more destabilizing effects. Much of this depends on the risk and protective factors present, as well as the presence of strengths and resilience. The hallmark of trauma is that the experience overwhelms one's normal capacity to cope, so the sequelae, or the aftereffects of the event, are subjective and unique for each individual. Roughly 50% of children and adolescents who experience trauma develop posttraumatic stress disorder (PTSD) (Afifi et al., 2011). The progression from experience to disorder is connected to the *type, duration,* and *severity* of the traumatic experiences, with rates of revictimizing being upward of a 69% chance for children with multiple forms of maltreatment (Pears, Kim, & Fisher, 2008). Intense and prolonged exposure is associated with more profound sequelae (Lawson, 2009). Often traumatic experiences are divided between those that are *interpersonal* in nature (neglect, physical abuse, sexual abuse) and those that are not (natural disasters, accidents). With interpersonal trauma, the experience of abuse from someone they are supposed to be able to trust and rely on can create sequelae know as *complex trauma*. As these experiences arise during development, the impact on the child's ability to manage emotions and develop safe and secure relationships can be profound (Cook et al., 2005). Estimates of substantiated childhood abuse reports in the United States hover around 1 million annually (D'Andrea et al., 2012).

Sequelae of Trauma in Children and Adolescents

The lasting impact of trauma can be felt across biological, psychological, behavioral, social, and spiritual dimensions for children and adolescents. Of course, each individual will be unique, but there are some general factors to consider. After the exploration of the sequelae you will find a set of case illustrations (Box 2.1).

Biological Sequelae

Traumatic experiences activate the natural "alarm" systems in the body. These natural stress response systems create the fight-flight-freeze responses that, over time, can lead to the development of somatic expressions of trauma such as gastrointestinal disorders, chronic pain, heart disease, immune disorders, and other issues (De Bellis & Zisk, 2014). Because neurological development will continue throughout childhood and adolescence, different developmental milestones and processes can be negatively affected, depending on the time that the traumatic experiences occur. The earlier the trauma occurs, the more difficulty a child may have in relation to developing basic neurological developmental functions, which then ripples into later developmental milestones (Davis et al., 2015). As with many psychosocial issues, the environment can offer multiple opportunities for protective factors, so a negative trajectory is not inevitable (Afifi & MacMillan, 2011).

The hypothalamic-pituitary-adrenal (HPA) system plays a key role in creating the stress reaction. The HPA system examines and determines whether a threat is present and then reacts if needed by releasing glucocorticoids, which trigger a neurochemical response. This in turn activates the prefrontal cortex, which subsequently activates other areas of the brain through the release of high dopamine receptors. This pattern ceases after the threat is

Box 2.1 Student Stories

Biological Sequelae

Amber is a 6-year-old girl in first grade. Amber witnessed her mother's violent death by gunshot when she was four years old. Since then, she has been moved around among family members with periods of homelessness. Amber is a quiet child who is withdrawn. Her teachers report that she is often found daydreaming in class, and teachers experience difficulty re-engaging her in the classroom. Amber is very timid around others and presents with hypervigilance, as evidenced by her sudden startle responses if someone approaches her from behind or if she hears a loud noise. Amber frequently asks to see the school nurse, reporting that her stomach hurts or that she has diarrhea.

Psychological and Behavioral Sequelae

Damian is a 13-year-old boy in seventh grade. Damian's mother and father had a tumultuous relationship throughout his childhood, characterized by physical and verbal abuse. His father has been incarcerated for several periods during his childhood. His father was released from jail five months ago, which has re-escalated the violence in his home. Damian gets into a lot of fights at school. Usually Damian reacts to other classmates with a lot of aggression for minor discretions, such as not letting Damian borrow a pencil or cutting in front of him in the hall. Damian has shared that he often struggles to stay asleep at night, which has gotten worse since his father's return to the home, and says that he often wakes up from nightmares. Damian is doing poorly in school and struggles to concentrate in class. In sixth grade Damian was referred to see a school social worker after expressing suicidal ideation, specifically wishing he didn't have to wake up in the morning.

Social and Spiritual Sequelae

Edgar is a nine-year-old boy who is in fourth grade. Edgar's father is an alcoholic who is inconsistent for his children. Edgar is usually responsible for taking care of his younger sister when they get home after school because his mother is busy tending to his father, who is often significantly inebriated. Edgar's family identifies as Catholic, and he goes to church his with mother and sister every Sunday. Edgar reports having a strong relationship with his father but has recently been asking more existential questions about his relationship with his father and family. During meetings with the school social worker, Edgar has communicated that he does not understand why God would choose this for his family and why God will not help his father get better. Edgar demonstrates awareness of how his father's alcoholism negatively affects his family and potentially Edgar's future. While Edgar and his mother find support in their church community, Edgar also feels isolated from other kids and struggles to find hope for his future.

extinguished. However, continued trauma can cause this pattern to continue, in which case the prefrontal cortex cannot regulate messages as intended, leaving the brain with high levels of dopamine, lower levels of glutamate, and increased gamma-aminobutyric acid (GABA) neurotransmitters. This dysregulation inhibits the prefrontal cortex's capacity to stop the HPA system's transmission of the stress response to the rest of the brain and body (Davis et al., 2014).

Cortisol is a hormone released by the adrenal glands when the HPA is activated. It allows the body to have the capacity to physically respond to distressing situations as it increases energy through the release of stored glucose and lipids (Davis et al., 2015). The amount of cortisol produced is what lets us know when to react to signs of danger. However, trauma exposure can cause the cortisol levels to be unbalanced, diminishing the ability to appropriately respond to a stressor, and may decrease the hippocampal volume (part of the limbic system), which can impede cognitive functioning (De Bellis & Zisk, 2014). In other words, if you think about a smoke alarm that is placed on the ceiling in a room, the smoke has to rise to a certain height to trip the alarm. With unbalanced levels of cortisol, the smoke level can be at a constant high level, meaning that very little is needed to trip the alarm. This is what hypervigilance looks like. Conversely, consistently low levels of cortisol require a greater than average increase to trip the alarm. In the first instance, the child may react to neutral stimuli as threats; in the latter, the child may not react to signs of danger, which leaves him or her vulnerable to revictimization.

The amygdala, which also emotionally categorizes the experience and communicates that response to the hippocampus, allows the person to address the threat in a behaviorally appropriate way, both the first time and the proceeding times after this threat is experienced. However, when there is chronic trauma, there are higher and longer rates of stressful stimuli, resulting in the dysregulation of the amygdala. This causes the amygdala to be hyperreactive, in which situation nonthreatening stimuli are treated as threatening, causing the limbic system to be inapplicably activated. It can also cause the hippocampal serotonin volume to be reduced, which may have a negative impact on a child's functioning and cognitions and cause an increased risk for psychiatric disorders such as depression and anxiety (Davis et al., 2014; De Bellis & Zisk, 2014).

The sympathetic nervous system (SNS), which is a main part of the fight-flight-freeze response, is also affected by chronic trauma. Those who have experienced childhood trauma have a higher risk for adverse health outcomes related to the ongoing, sustained activation of the SNS system (Anda et al., 2006). These problems can show up in children and adolescents with somatic problems such as gastrointestinal difficulties, heart disease, asthma, cancer, and obesity (Dantzer et al., 2008). As noted in the results from the Adverse Childhood Experiences Study, these health risks are connected to atypical, increased, and sustained levels of norepinephrine, neuroendocrine, serotonin, and cortisol levels.

Children and adolescents can also be negatively affected by childhood trauma in terms of attention, executive functioning, and IQ, particularly when the trauma occurs before age nine (Pears, Kim, & Fisher, 2008). The effect of intellectual functioning in relation to physical trauma may be due to the impact that the trauma has on the physical brain. Trauma related to neglect affects intellectual functioning in that it does not allow for development of "age-appropriate intellectual abilities" because there is a lack of learning opportunities owing to a decrease in opportunities for a child to learn to connect and interact with others. Because intelligence is seen to have a particular connection with academic performance, understanding the connection between trauma and neurobiology is particularly important for those in school settings. The impact of trauma on academic performance will be addressed more in depth in Chapter 3.

Psychological and Behavioral Sequelae

Early child maltreatment inhibits a child's ability to experience secure attachments, which can have ripple effects into adolescence and beyond. Secure attachments that exemplify safety and security allow a child to gain the emotional skills necessary to navigate the world, thus enabling the child to develop constructive coping mechanisms to employ when there is a negative interaction or experience. Without this foundation, coping mechanisms may become maladaptive and cause other psychosocial problems. Thus, children who have experienced child maltreatment are already in an atmosphere of stress and have not learned the appropriate and adaptive ways to cope with stressors, causing a higher risk for developing mental health disorders (Milot et al., 2010). Children who experience interpersonal trauma such as abuse and neglect may show symptoms of avoidance and hyperarousal, as well as act as if they are re-experiencing the trauma. These psychological and behavioral symptoms show up in their emotions and actions that may not be easily identifiable as a trauma reaction (D'Andrea et al., 2012).

Mood and anxiety disorders affect 40% of children with trauma histories (Copeland et al., 2007). In young children, this can be seen as generalized fear, regression to earlier developmental stages, separation anxiety, irritability, hypervigilance, and rumination. These *internalizing disorders* are often not identified as trauma sequelae, nor are they flagged as problems in school settings because they are inwardly focused experiences of distress that usually do not become overt behavioral issues in the classroom. *Externalizing disorders* are more commonly the focus of classroom attention, and these children can be disruptive owing to a variety of behaviors that include not paying attention and being hyperactive, defiant, oppositional, aggressive, or a bully (O'Hare, 2016). In school-aged children, re-enactment of the trauma themes can be externalized in their play during class, physical education, and school convocations and on the playground and at other unexpected places.

Affect regulation, whether demonstrated in internalizing or externalizing behaviors, is seen in a child's aggression, withdrawal, guilt, and somatic symptoms such as headache and stomachache, along with problems concentrating and learning (Hunt, Slack, & Berger, 2017). Flat affect, explosive anger, and inappropriate affect are also common indicators of the child's inability to regulate affect (D'Andrea et al., 2012). As children become adolescents, if these issues are unaddressed, they may lead to acting-out behaviors that are dangerous, coping behaviors that are self-harming, detachment from others, increased shame and guilt, and intense feelings that can be scary (Peh et al., 2017). Sleep and eating disorders, personality-related problems, confusion around sense of self and identity, increased dissociation, sexual difficulties, mood and anxiety disorders, suicidal thoughts and impulses, and hyperactivity and hyperarousal are common adolescent challenges (Lawson, 2009). Many struggling with affect regulation in these situations can develop substance use disorders if they turn to alcohol and other drugs as a form of chemical self-regulation (Alvarez-Alonso et al., 2016).

The ability of children and those around them to help master regulation of affect is seen as a key mediator between childhood trauma and the development of mental and behavioral health disorders (Jennissen et al., 2016); learning to regulate affect is a key task of childhood that is interrupted by traumatic experiences. In the extreme, adolescents whose aggression and acting-out behaviors meet the criteria for conduct disorder due to engaging in physical or sexual violence, bullying, stealing, or destruction of public property are more likely to have experienced child maltreatment (Afifi et al., 2011). Therefore, understanding that children and adolescents who act out behaviorally are likely to lack the skills to control their behavior and are not necessarily choosing to "be bad" is crucial to formulating a solution.

Social and Spiritual Sequelae

Exposure to trauma can affect not only the child's brain development, mental health, and behavior but also the child's ability to engage with others socially. Abuse and neglect by someone the child is supposed to be able to trust means that the boundaries of that relationship have been violated; this can be a caregiver, family member, friend, teacher, religious leader, coach, or other community member. Determining whom to trust and how to set healthy boundaries are the foundation of social relationships, and successfully navigating these issues are negatively affected for many children and adolescents (D'Andrea et al., 2012; Kernhof, Kaufhold, & Grabhorn, 2008). Important social skills such as the ability to read social cues, understand how to engage in social situations, and intuit the perspective of another person have been found to be inhibited by child maltreatment and lead to social isolation (Elliott et al., 2005). It is understandable that children who can be emotionally unpredictable, aggressive, hypervigilant, and socially inappropriate may have a difficult time navigating playground politics and forming and maintaining friendships because other children may find this behavior off-putting, confusing, or even scary. Equally concerning is the child who is socially withdrawn, extremely shy, rejected by peers, a "loner," and without school friends.

Spirituality and religiosity can serve as a protective factor for mental health disorders (Howell & Miller-Graff, 2014; Levin, 2010) because many spiritual and religious traditions offer practices and rituals that can be used to cope with adversity (Farley, 2007). However, childhood maltreatment can cause a child or adolescent to turn away from family traditions and practices (Feinson & Meir, 2015). Childhood abuse can have a negative impact on trust in God or a higher power, causing anger and distress that can last long into adulthood (Gall, Basque, Damasceno-Scott, & Vardy, 2007). Effects of child maltreatment on spirituality may not be evident until later in adulthood when individuals decide on religious practices for themselves instead of following family norms, and a spiritual connection can provide a sense of focus and certainty in unstable times (Howell & Miller-Graff, 2014; Springer, Sheridan, Kuo, & Carnes, 2007). Spirituality has also been shown to be connected to social supports, particularly for adolescents and emerging adults, who can benefit from a formal community that surrounds religious institutions, particularly when family connections are not safe (Howell & Miller-Graff, 2014). This has specific implications for faith-based school settings and for secular schools where family faith traditions are considered. Children who are socially isolated, have difficulty forming friends, or have sudden changes in spirituality or religiosity may be demonstrating the sequelae of an adverse childhood experience.

Strengths Perspective

A counterpoint to any discussion on trauma must emphasize that students do succeed in school despite their complex histories by drawing on their internal and external resources. This approach is important for several reasons. As Dennis Saleebey (2012) has maintained for many years, clients are best served when social workers are mindful of their clients' strengths. This means eliciting information about client capacities, abilities, and networks, which De Jong and Berg (2007) referred to as a solution focus, and avoiding a problem-saturated narrative or victim mindset. Not concentrating on the deficits of a situation allows attention to be directed toward individual, interpersonal, social, and environment protective factors (Corcoran & Nichols-Casebolt, 2004). Thus, the aim is to demonstrate respect for the whole person and to set the stage for a collaborative working relationship with people and their formal community institutions and informal social supports. See Box 2.2 for discussion of the moderating influence of resilience.

Box 2.2 Resilience—The Moderating Influence

Why is it that some students with the same ACEs do not develop traumatic symptoms like others? Researchers usually look for an intervening variable—some factor that serves as an intermediating influence between the presumed cause and the probable effect. Certainly, past trauma can make a child more vulnerable to adverse experiences, but can resilience make a child less vulnerable?

Resilience has sometimes been described as a steeling response that reduces vulnerability to later stress (Rutter, 2006). Some consider it the ability to adapt to circumstances that threaten the survival of a living system (Masten, 2012). Sometimes it has been called the ability to harness resources that sustain one's well-being (Panter-Brick & Leckman, 2013) or the ability to grow and even thrive in the face of adversity (Connor & Davidson, 2003; Davydoff et al., 2010). The National Scientific Council on the Developing Child (2015) puts it this way:

Whether it is considered an outcome, a process, or a capacity, the essence of resilience is a positive, adaptive response in the face of significant adversity. It is neither an immutable trait nor a resource that can be used up. . . . Stated simply, resilience transforms potentially toxic stress into tolerable stress. (p. 3)

Connor and Davidson (2003) developed the most widely used scale to measure resilience and identified five dimensions of resilience. The scale has 25 items measured on a five-point scale. They found that the scale measured five factors: (1) personal competence and tenacity, (2) trust in one's instincts and tolerance of negative affect, (3) positive acceptance of change and secure relationships, (4) sense of control and resourcefulness, and (5) spirituality and the ability to find meaning. In 2007, Campbell-Sills and Stein produced an empirically derived version with just ten items. Both the full-length and the ten-item scale have been adapted for Spanish speakers (Crespo, Fernández-Lansac, & Soberón, 2014; Soler Sánchez, de Pedro, & García-Izquierdo, 2016). Finally, Vaishnavi, Connor, and Davidson (2007) created a theoretically derived version with just two items

("Able to adapt to change" and "Tend to bounce back after illness or hardship") to create an abbreviated version of the scale.

Ding and associates (2017) surveyed more than 6,000 Chinese youths in middle school and high school and asked about five types of ACEs: (a) emotional abuse, (b) physical abuse, (c) sexual abuse, (d) emotional neglect, and (e) physical neglect. They found that resilience, as measured by the Connor–Davidson Resilience Scale (CD-RISC), moderated the association between trauma exposure and depressive symptoms. Poole and colleagues (2017) examined more than 4,000 Canadian adults about ACEs and also found that their scores on the CD-RISC moderated depressive symptoms. Schulz and associates (2014) surveyed more than 2,000 adults in Northern Europe and found that while child maltreatment was significantly associated with major depressive disorder, resilience moderated its effects so that those with the highest resilience scores were far less likely to be depressed.

Resilience does not just moderate depression among those experiencing ACEs. Wingo, Ressler, and Brady (2014) studied more than 2,000 inner-city adults in the southeastern United States and found that resilience also moderated their use of alcohol and illicit substance use. Logan-Greene and associates (2014) studied the prevalence of ACEs in more than 19,000 adults in the northwestern United States. They found that resilience, as measured by sleep quality, social-emotional support, and life satisfaction, significantly reduced the number of poor physical health days and poor mental health days reported per month.

—Jim Raines

What does all this mean for school social workers? It suggests that social workers wanting to take a strengths perspective must always inquire about students' assets or resilience. This is especially true for students with a high number of ACEs (i.e., four or more). If we never collect information about students' resilience, it is impossible to harness it.

Conclusion

Even with the changes in the understanding of the psychosocial impact of trauma in the Trauma- and Stressor-Related Disorders in the DSM-5, which considers symptoms in early childhood and adolescents (American Psychiatric Association, 2013), many trauma researchers feel that the current formulation of the PTSD diagnosis falls short of capturing the true picture (Bremness & Polzin, 2014). This can explain why so many children exposed to abuse, neglect, and other forms of trauma do not meet criteria for a PTSD diagnosis and are diagnosed with an anxiety or mood disorder instead. At the core of psychological and behavioral problems are a specific cluster of symptoms that reflect an inability to regulate emotions, behaviors, attention, relationships, identity, and somatic reactions that result from their exposure to traumatic experiences (Bremness & Polzin, 2014; van der Kolk, 2005). Bearing this in mind, along with a strengths perspective, will help all those in a school setting respond in a trauma-informed manner.

Resources

In 2018 the US government separated some children and parents crossing the American southern border, resulting in traumatic experiences that will have negative long-term educational effects. Multiple professional groups published official statements objecting to this policy, some describing it as child abuse and a violation of the UN Convention on the Rights of Children. In years to come, some of these children may be enrolled in public schools, creating a wave of children who have experienced a unique trauma and a greater need for a trauma-informed approach for responding to their learning needs. More information and resources on immigration, separation, and childhood trauma are available on the following websites.

Academy of American Pediatricians: https://www.aap.org/en-us/about-the-aap/aap-press-room/Pages/AAPStatementOpposingBorderSecurityandImmigrationReformAct.aspx

American Psychological Association: http://www.apa.org/advocacy/immigration/index.aspx

American School Counselor Association: https://www.prweb.com/releases/2018/06/prweb15577365.htm

National Association of Social Workers: https://www.prweb.com/releases/2018/06/prweb15577365.htm

School Social Work Association of America: https://www.prweb.com/releases/2018/06/prweb15577365.htm

References

Afifi, T. O., & MacMillan, H. L. (2011). Resilience following child maltreatment: A review of protective factors. *Canadian Journal of Psychiatry, 56,* 266–272.

Afifi, T. O., MacMillan, H. L., Asmundson, G. J. G., Piertrzak, R. H., & Sareen, J. (2011). An examination of the relation between conduct disorder, childhood and adulthood traumatic events, and posttraumatic stress disorder in a nationally representative sample. *Journal of Psychiatric Research, 45*(12), 1564–1572.

Alvarez-Alonso, M. J., Jurado-Barba, R., Martinez-Martin, N., Espin-Jaime, J. C., Bolaños-Porrero, C., Ordoñez-Franco, A., . . . Rubio, G. (2016). Association between maltreatment and polydrug use among adolescents. *Child Abuse & Neglect, 51,* 379–389.

American Psychiatric Association. (2013). *Diagnostic and statistical manual of mental disorders* (5th ed.). Washington, DC: Author.

Anda, R. F., Felitti, V. J., Bremner, J. D., Walker, J. D., Whitfield, C., Perry, B. D., Dube, S. R., & Giles, W. H. (2006). The enduring effects of abuse and related adverse experiences in childhood: A convergence of evidence from neurobiology and epidemiology. *European Archives of Psychiatry and Clinical Neuroscience, 256*(3), 174–186.

Bremness, A., & Polzin, W. (2014). Commentary: Developmental trauma disorder: A missed opportunity in DSM V. *Journal of the Canadian Academy of Child and Adolescent Psychiatry, 23*(2), 142–145.

Campbell-Sills, L., & Stein, M. B. (2007). Psychometric analysis and refinement of the Connor-Davidson Resilience Scale (CD-RISC): Validation of a 10-item measure of resilience. *Journal of Traumatic Stress, 20*(6), 1019–1028.

Connor, K. M., & Davidson, J. R. T. (2003). Development of a new resilience scale: The Connor-Davidson Resilience Scale (CD-RISC). *Depression & Anxiety, 18,* 76–82.

Cook, A., Spinazzola, J., Ford, J., Lanktree, C., Blaustein, M., Cloitre, M., . . . van der Kolk, B. (2005). Complex trauma in children and adolescents. *Psychiatric Annals, 35,* 390–398.

Copeland, W. E., Keeler, G., Angold, A., & Costello, E. J. (2007). Traumatic events and posttraumatic stress in childhood. *Archives of General Psychiatry, 64,* 577–584.

Corcoran, J., & Nichols-Casebolt, A. (2004). Risk and resilience ecological framework for assessment and goal formulation. *Child and Adolescent Social Work Journal 21*(3), 211–235.

Crespo, M., Fernández-Lansac, V., & Soberón, C. (2014). Adaptación Española de la "Escala de resiliencia de Connor-Davidson" (CD-RISC) en situaciones de estrés crónico. *Psicología Conductual: Revista Internacional Clínica y de la Salud, 22*(2), 219–238.

D'Andrea, W., Ford, J., Stolbach, B., Spinazzola, J., & van der Kolk, B. A. (2012). Understanding interpersonal trauma in children: Why we need a developmentally appropriate trauma diagnosis. *American Journal of Orthopsychiatry, 82*(2), 187–200.

Dantzer, R., O'Connor, J. C., Freund, G. G., Johnson, R. W., & Kelley, K. W. (2008). From inflammation to sickness and depression: When the immune system subjugates the brain. *Nature Reviews Neuroscience, 9*(1), 46–56.

Davis, A. S., Moss, L. E., Nogin, M. M., & Webb, N. E. (2015). Neuropsychology of child maltreatment and implications for school psychologists. *Psychology in the Schools, 52*(1), 77–91.

Davydov, D. M., Stewart, R., Ritchie, K., & Chaudieu, I. (2010). Resilience and mental health. *Clinical Psychology Review, 30*(5), 479–495.

De Bellis, M. D., & Zisk, A. (2014). The biological effects of childhood trauma. *Child and Adolescent Psychiatric Clinics of North America, 23*(2), 185–222.

De Jong, P., & Berg, I. K. (2007). *Interviewing for solutions* (3rd ed.). Pacific Grove, CA: Brooks/Cole.

Ding, H., Han, J., Zhang, M., Wang, K., Gong, J., & Yang, S. (2017). Moderating and mediating effects of resilience between childhood trauma and depressive symptoms in Chinese children. *Journal of Affective Disorders, 211*, 130–135.

Elliott, G. C., Cunningham, S. M., Linder, M., Colangelo, M., & Gross, M. (2005). Child physical abuse and self-perceived social isolation among adolescents. *Journal of Interpersonal Violence, 20*, 1663–1684.

Farley, Y. R. (2007). Making the connection: Spirituality, trauma, and resilience. *Journal of Religion and Spirituality in Social Work, 26*(1), 1–15.

Feinson, M., & Meir, A. (2015). Exploring mental health consequences of childhood abuse and the relevance of religiosity. *Journal of Interpersonal Violence, 30*(3), 499–521.

Gall, T. L., Basque, V., Damasceno-Scott, M., & Vardy, G. (2007). Spirituality and the current adjustment of adult survivors of childhood sexual abuse. *Journal for the Scientific Study of Religion, 46*, 101–117.

Howell, K. H., & Miller-Graff, L. E. (2014). Protective factors associated with resilient functioning in young adulthood after childhood exposure to violence. *Child Abuse & Neglect, 38*, 1985–1994.

Hunt, T. K. A., Slack, K. S., & Berger, L. M. (2017). Adverse childhood experiences and behavioral problems in middle childhood. *Child Abuse & Neglect, 67*, 391–402.

Jennissen, S., Holl, J., Mai, H., Wolff, S., & Barnow, S. (2016). Emotion dysregulation mediates the relationship between child maltreatment and psychopathology: A structural equation model. *Child Abuse & Neglect, 62*, 51–62.

Kernhof, K., Kaufhold, J., & Grabhorn, R. (2008). Object relations and interpersonal problems in sexually abused female patients: An empirical study with SCORS and the HP. *Journal of Personality Assessment, 90*, 44–51.

Lawson, D. M. (2009). Understanding and treating children who experience interpersonal maltreatment: Empirical findings. *Journal of Counseling & Development, 87*(2), 204–215.

Levin, J. (2010). Religion and mental health: Theory and research. *International Journal of Applied Psychoanalytic Studies, 7*(2), 102–115.

Logan-Greene, P., Green, S., Nurius, P. S., & Longhi, D. (2014). Distinct contributions of adverse childhood experiences and resilience resources: A cohort analysis of adult physical and mental health. *Social Work in Health Care, 53*(8), 776–797.

Masten, A. S. (2012). Risk and resilience in development. In P. D. Zelazo (Ed.), *The Oxford handbook of developmental psychology* (Vol. 2). New York, NY: Oxford University Press.

Milot, T., Éthier, L. S., St-Laurent, D., & Provost, M. A. (2010). The role of trauma symptoms in the development of behavioral problems in maltreated preschoolers. *Child Abuse & Neglect, 34*(4), 225–234.

National Scientific Council on the Developing Child. (2015). *Supportive relationships and active skill-building strengthen the foundations of resilience: Working paper 13.* Retrieved from http://www.developingchild.harvard.edu

O'Hare, T. (2016). *Essential skills of social work practice: Assessment, intervention, and evaluation.* New York: NY: Oxford University Press.

Panter-Brick, C., & Leckman, J. F. (2013). Editorial commentary: Resilience in child development—Interconnected pathways to wellbeing. *Journal of Child Psychology and Psychiatry, 54*(4), 333–336.

Pears, K. C., Kim, H. K., & Fisher, P. A. (2008). Psychosocial and cognitive functioning of children with specific profiles of maltreatment. *Child Abuse & Neglect, 32*(10), 958–971.

Peh, C. X., Shahwan, S., Fauziana, R., Mahesh, M. V., Sambasivam, R., Zhang, Y., Ong, S., Chong, S., & Subramaniam, M. (2017). Emotional dysregulation as a mechanism linking child maltreatment exposure and self-harm behaviors in adolescents. *Child Abuse & Neglect, 67*, 383–390.

Poole, J. C., Dobson, K. S., & Pusch, D. (2017). Anxiety among adults with a history of childhood adversity: Psychological resilience moderates the indirect effect of emotion dysregulation. *Journal of Affective Disorders, 217*, 144–152.

Rutter, M. (2006). Implications of resilience concepts for scientific understanding. In B. M. Lester, A. Masten, & B. McEwen (Eds.), *Resilience in children* (pp. 1–12). Boston, MA: Blackwell Publishing.

Saleebey, D. (Ed.) (2012). *The strengths perspective in social work practice* (6th ed.). New York, NY: Pearson Education.

Sandman, C. A., Davis, E. P., Buss, C., & Glynn, L. (2012). Exposure to prenatal psychobiological stress exerts programming influences on the mother and her fetus. *Neuroendocrinology, 95*(1), 8–21.

Schulz, A., Becker, M., Van der Auwera, S., Barnow, S., Appel, K., Mahler, J., . . . Grabe, H. J. (2014). The impact of childhood trauma on depression: Does resilience matter? Population-based results from the study of health in Pomerania. *Journal of Psychosomatic Research, 77*(2), 97–103.

Soler Sánchez, M. I., de Pedro, M. M., & García-Izquierdo, M. (2016). Propiedades psicométricas de la versión española de la escala de resiliencia de 10 ítems de Connor-Davidson (CD-RISC 10) en una muestra multiocupacional. *Revista Latinoamericana de Psicología, 48*(3), 159–166.

Springer, K. W., Sheridan, J., Kuo, D., & Carnes, M. (2007). Long-term physical and mental health consequences of childhood physical abuse: Results from a large population-based sample of men and women. *Child Abuse & Neglect, 31*, 517–530.

US Department of Health and Human Services, National Center for Injury Prevention and Control, Division of Violence Prevention. (2016). *About the CDC-Kaiser ACE Study*. Retrieved from https://www.cdc.gov/violenceprevention/acestudy/about.html

Vaishnavi, S., Connor, K., & Davidson, J. R. T. (2007). An abbreviated version of the Connor-Davidson Resilience Scale (CD-RISC), the CD-RISC2: Psychometric properties and applications in psychopharmacological trials. *Psychiatry Research, 152*, 293–297.

van der Kolk, B. (2005). Developmental trauma disorder: Toward a rational diagnosis for children with complex trauma histories. *Psychiatric Annals, 35*(5), 401–408.

Wingo, A. P., Ressler, K. J., & Bradley, B. (2014). Resilience characteristics mitigate tendency for harmful alcohol and illicit drug use in adults with a history of childhood abuse: A cross-sectional study of 2024 inner-city men and women. *Journal of Psychiatric Research, 51*, 93–99.

3

The Impact of Trauma on Learning
PTSD, ADHD, and SPED

> Children who have been subjected to ongoing abuse and neglect in the context of their primary relationships and whose family environments have lacked adequate support have been found to differ in their neurological and neurobiological development from children who have not been abused or neglected. (van der Kolk & Courtois, 2005, p. 386)

Research shows that children and adolescents who experience abuse and neglect have lower learning outcomes, higher rates of learning difficulties, and higher rates of mental health disorders and behavioral challenges than children without these traumatic experiences (Holmes et al., 2015; Perfect et al., 2016). This chapter explores some of the common social, emotional, behavioral, and academic issues seen in children who experience trauma. Information is provided to help school social workers with the process of differential diagnosis and differentiation among symptoms of posttraumatic stress disorder (PTSD), attention deficit hyperactivity disorder (ADHD), and the cognitive and intellectual issues that require special education.

Impact of Trauma on Learning

Exposure to traumatic events in childhood can lead to negative effects on the ability to pay attention and maintain consciousness (D'Andrea et al., 2012), which are crucial to learning. This is why early detection of traumatic distress is so crucial for interrupting the path of academic difficulties (Gonzalez et al., 2016). Trauma triggers can lead to a dissociative state, which means that the child is not fully present in the current moment, but brought back to a previous unsafe time. Triggers can bring about flashbacks, which are vivid memories that can feel as if they are currently happening. When a child is in a dissociative or flashback state, the child's behavior can be confusing to others, and the child is unable to tune into what is happening in the moment. In this state, the child is not ready to absorb any new information.

Because of issues with attention, learning difficulties are more likely to arise for children who have experienced trauma. According to the research on school outcomes (Perfect et al., 2016), the most common difficulties are:

- Lower intelligence test (IQ) scores
- Impaired memory—working, visual, spatial, and verbal
- Poorer verbal ability
- Language disorders
- Poorer standardized test performance—particularly on math and reading
- Higher rates of discipline referrals
- Excessive absences
- Inability to successfully complete a grade
- Lower academic engagement in general
- Higher suspension and dropout rates

Often these issues become the "problem," and the fact that the child has experienced trauma, or is currently, is overlooked. School social workers can remind the adults working with kids who have these issues that trauma may be a factor in the child's school performance and that by treating the trauma, some of these issues can be ameliorated. Exploring the type and number of traumatic experiences is also important because some research has shown that a child who has had multiple types of traumatic incidents may require more extensive treatment (Holt, Finkelhor, & Kantor, 2007).

Impact of Trauma on Social Interactions, Emotions, and Behaviors

The bio-psycho-social-spiritual sequelae of trauma were explored in depth in Chapter 2. This section will discuss the implications of these challenges in the context of learning. School-related behavioral problems in traumatized children can show up as early as preschool, with consequences such as expulsion for those children who are particularly aggressive and difficult to manage in the classroom (Gilliam, 2005). For other children, their expressions of trauma may be more internalizing than externalizing, and they develop symptoms that appear more physical than emotional (e.g., stomach aches). In general, exposure to traumatic events in childhood more than doubles the chances of developing mental health disorders (Norman et al., 2012). Much of these internalizing and externalizing problematic behaviors arise from negative thoughts about themselves and the world (e.g., "no one likes me" or "I'm bad") as they try to make meaning of the trauma on their own (Holmes et al., 2015). They become the students in the classroom who have overall difficulties in socializing with their peers (Berthelot et al., 2015; Holt, Finkelhor, & Kantor, 2007) and are at greater risk later on, in adolescence, of turning to binge drinking (Shin, Edwards, & Heeren, 2009), drug use, and risky sexual behavior (Sege & Amaya-Jackson, 2017).

These kinds of social, emotional, and behavioral difficulties are observed by teachers who can refer these children to school social workers. School social workers can help all the adults in their school understand these behaviors as communication. This is a child who needs support and services, but this type of child is often overlooked if internalizing and is often sent out of the classroom if externalizing. Aggressiveness and hyperactivity tend to draw the most attention in a classroom (Lamers-Winkelman et al., 2012), and diagnoses of ADHD and conduct disorder are the most common (Sege & Amaya-Jackson, 2017), which may also overlook the presence of trauma.

ADHD and PTSD

Many children diagnosed with ADHD also have histories of trauma. Inattention and hyperactivity may appear to be the primary features, but they are often co-occurring symptoms with trauma. Consequently, children are often misdiagnosed with ADHD when PTSD is the presenting problem (Biederman et al., 2013; Grasso et al., 2009). Research has shown that child maltreatment increases the chances of developing ADHD by upward of five times of children who do not experience abuse (Sanderud, Murphy, & Elkit,

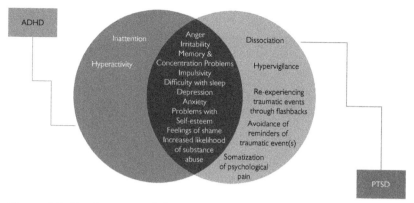

Figure 3.1 Overlapping and divergent characteristics of attention deficit hyperactivity disorder (ADHD) and posttraumatic stress disorder (PTSD).

2016). The trauma goes undetected and therefore untreated in these children. Understanding the differences and similarities between these two disorders is crucial in school social work so that each child's needs are met. While a full set of criteria for each disorder can be found in the *Diagnostic and Statistical Manual of Mental Disorders* (DSM) (American Psychiatric Association, 2013), we will explore the overlapping symptoms here.

Inattention and hyperactivity are hallmarks of ADHD, which can appear very similar to the experiences of dissociation and arousal or hypervigilance in PTSD. Anger and irritability also overlap in these two sets of diagnostic criteria, along with memory and concentration problems, impulsivity, and difficulty with sleep. There are often accompanying issues with depression, anxiety, self-esteem, and shame because of the effects of coping with the symptoms. Finally, with both PTSD and ADHD, there is an increased likelihood of developing a substance use disorder (Harstad & Levy, 2014; Najavits & Hein, 2013). Key differences between these two sets of symptoms are found in the presence of re-experiencing traumatic events through flashbacks, avoidance of reminders of the events, and somatization of psychological pain that occur in PTSD but not ADHD (American Psychiatric Association, 2013). Figure 3.1 depicts the overlapping and divergent characteristics of ADHD and PTSD.

Conduct Disorder and PTSD

In addition to ADHD, conduct disorder is a common diagnosis for children and adolescents who have had traumatic experiences (Afifi et al.,

---

2011; Bernhard et al., 2018). While the criteria for PTSD and conduct disorder do not overlap as much as ADHD and PTSD, conduct disorder can be understood as ways of acting out the trauma or demonstrating behavior that has been modeled for them by others. According to the DSM (American Psychiatric Association, 2013), children and adolescents who meet criteria for conduct disorder engage in four general categories of behaviors:

1. Aggression acted out on others. This behavior can include bullying, threating, and intimidating behavior. The child will start fights with others and may or may not use a weapon to cause harm. Physical cruelty can be exhibited to both animals and humans and can include forced sexual interactions.
2. Disregard for and destruction of property. This is done through destructive behavior such as setting fires or other deliberate means.
3. Lying, deceiving, and stealing. These behaviors include breaking and entering the homes or vehicles of others to obtain their property, shoplifting, forgery, and lying to secure material good or favors from others.
4. Violation of rules and norms for age and stage of development. In these cases, the child or adolescent will stay out beyond curfew at night, run away from home and be gone overnight, and skip school.

In all these cases, the behavior causes significant problems with academic and social function, making it difficult for the child to be successful in school. Given that anger and irritability are symptoms of PTSD, the aggression exhibited by a child who has conduct disorder may be connected to the need to self-protect and act out toward others before getting hurt by adults or classmates at school. In working with a child or adolescent who is showing signs of conduct disorder, the school social worker should screen for past or current experiences of trauma. In some cases, the behavior will be explained by the trauma, and addressing it through treatment can help the child change these behaviors and possibly avoid further educational difficulties or even entrance into the juvenile justice system (Bernhard et al., 2018).

Running behind any mental health disorder is the principle of epigenetics. Box 3.1 explains the linkages among genetics, environment, and mental

Box 3.1 Epigenetics and Mental Health

Social workers take a biopsychosocial approach to assessment. This has sometimes been misinterpreted to mean a biological, psychological, and social approach to assessment, indicating that each domain is separate and distinct from the others, but that a complete assessment will include all three domains. The study of epigenetics is beginning to shed light on how all three domains are interconnected, circular, and impossible to separate.

Epigenetics is the study of potentially heritable changes in how genes express themselves that does not involve changes to the underlying DNA sequence (Nestler, 2016). Changes in gene expression are changes to the phenotype, but not the genotype (Bagot & Meaney, 2010; Lester, Marsit, & Bromer, 2014). A genotype is the set of genes in our DNA that is responsible for a specific trait, while a phenotype is the set of characteristics that express that trait. For example, monozygotic twins occur approximately once in every 250 births. Chances are that if you've known a set of identical twins well, you've noticed subtle differences in how their common DNA is expressed. They have slightly different heights, weights, and personalities—even their fingerprints are different! The difference between genotypes and phenotypes could be compared to the difference between words and how they are spoken. From a mental health perspective, it may be compared to the difference between a mental disorder and how it manifests. For example, some clients with depression will appear sad and morose, while other clients may act irritable and agitated.

Epigenetic changes are caused by a host of factors: prenatal nutrition, maternal exposure to toxic substances, abusive parenting practices, and environmental hardships. There is evidence that children born during the Dutch famine (1944–1945) were at increased risk for coronary heart disease and obesity (Painter, Roseboom, & Bleker, 2005). Epigenetic changes could help explain the connection between adverse childhood experiences (ACEs) and current biopsychosocial functioning in adults. Those who experienced four or more ACEs had 1.5 times more physical inactivity and severe obesity; 2 to 4 times the risk for smoking and poor health; 4 to 12 times the risk for alcoholism, drug abuse, depression, and suicide attempt; and more than 50 sexual partners (Felitti et al., 1998).

Today neuroscientists are discovering that both acute and chronic stress from bullying (Zarate-Garza et al., 2017), child abuse, and other ACEs are implicated in a wide variety of psychiatric problems, including aggression, anxiety, autism spectrum disorder, bipolar disorder, depression, posttraumatic stress disorder, and substance abuse (Beach et al., 2013; Heinrich et al., 2015; Montalvo-Ortiz, Gelernter, Hudziak, & Kaufman, 2016; Mehta et al., 2013; Nemeroff & Binder, 2014; Wong et al., 2014).

Moreover, there is emerging scientific evidence that epigenetic changes are transgenerational (Nestler, 2016; Oh et al., 2015; Pariante, 2014). From a social justice perspective, this may eventually provide a biological explanation for the concept of historical trauma in oppressed groups like African Americans (Henderson, Acquaye-Doyle, Waites, & Howard, 2016) and Native Americans (Brave Heart, Chase, Elkins, & Altschul, 2011; Ehlers, Gizer, Gilder, Ellingson, & Yehuda, 2013; Nutton & Fast, 2015). Thus, epigenetics has the potential to end the nature versus nurture debate in human development. From a social work perspective, it's not the person in the environment, it's also the environment in the person. The influences are reciprocal and intertwined just like a strand of DNA (Raines, 2019).

health that are crucial for understanding how traumatic events affect a child's growth, development, and learning.

Relationship Between Trauma and Special Education Placement

According to research conducted by the National Child Traumatic Stress Network (2008), one out of every four children will have been exposed to a traumatic event that can affect learning and behavior. Children who have experienced childhood trauma are more likely to have higher rates of school absences, increased likelihood to drop out of school, and more suspensions and expulsions. Early childhood exposure to trauma can also impair learning. Research indicates that traumatic events, especially chronic trauma, can adversely affect a child's ability to concentrate and organize information and affect memory and cognition. Trauma can also cause emotional and physical distress, evidenced by manifestation of somatic symptoms, poor emotional control, hypervigilance, and impulsive behavior (National Child Traumatic Stress Network, 2008). While the prevalence and implications of childhood trauma are significant, many of these children go unnoticed and underserved in our education system based on criteria outlined in the Individuals with Disabilities in Education Act (IDEA).

The Individuals with Disabilities Education Act was created to address the needs of youths with disabilities in the education system. Of the 13 conditions for coverage under IDEA, "emotional disturbance" is the category that comes closest to describing the presentation of children with trauma symptoms. The current definition of "emotional disturbance" dictates that an emotional disturbance is a condition, over a long period of time, to a marked degree, that negatively affects a student's educational performance. This category includes several mental health diagnoses, such as schizophrenia, bipolar disorder, anxiety, and depression; however, it includes an exclusionary clause for youths who are "socially maladjusted," which often includes traumatized youths (Barnett, 2012).

Research estimates that one in five, or 20%, of children present with a mental health condition that causes at least a mild educational impairment. However, only 1% of the school-aged population receive special education supports under the "emotional disturbance" classification. The current definition of "emotional disturbance" is critiqued as being too vague and subjective, as evidenced by inconsistent use and application across districts and states (Barnett, 2012). The definition fails to identify the specific needs of children exposed to trauma. As a result, many traumatized children go undetected and are not referred for special education services to address their academic needs, which can have long-term impacts on their education and future (Winder, 2015).

A secondary analysis of the National Survey of Children's Health (2011/ 12) examined adverse family experiences, child mental health, and educational outcomes (Porche, Costello, & Rosen-Reynoso, 2016). The researchers found that children with higher numbers of adverse family experiences were more likely to have higher numbers of mental health diagnoses, and those children were less likely to be engaged in school, more likely to be retained in grade, and more likely to have an Individualized Education Plan.

A systematic review of the empirical literature on cognitive, academic, and social-emotional-behavioral outcomes of children and adolescents exposed to traumatic events revealed several important findings (Perfect et al., 2016). Studies on cognitive functioning found lower IQ scores, impaired memory, and lower verbal ability (Perfect et al., 2016). Negative academic outcomes were found in the areas of discipline, school dropout, and attendance (Perfect et al., 2016). Research on teacher reports of social-emotional-learning functioning found clinically significant externalizing behaviors such as classroom disruption, aggression, hyperactivity, and defiance (Perfect et al., 2016). Studies also indicated that students exposed to traumatic events had higher levels of internalizing symptoms (sadness, depression, anxiety, withdrawn, and low self-esteem) compared with those who had not (Perfect et al., 2016). Even experiencing extreme weather events, witnessing accidental death on school grounds, and having incarcerated parents have been found to be negatively associated with academic outcomes (Porche, Costello, & Rosen-Reynoso, 2016).

An important implication for school social workers is that negative educational outcomes begin to appear in childhood, providing school social workers with a rationale for helping to develop trauma-informed schools. More important, research indicates that there is a positive association between children's mental health services and academic outcomes (Becker, Brandt, Stephan, & Chorpita, 2014).

Student Study Teams

To be eligible for special education services, federal law requires a multifaceted, nondiscriminatory evaluation, ensuring an individual and comprehensive assessment of the child's needs (IDEA, 2004). The evaluation must be conducted by a multidisciplinary team with knowledge of the child and in the area of the suspected disability (IDEA, 2004).

Consideration of the multifaceted nature of trauma is a critical factor that school social workers must bring to student evaluations (Mirabito & Callahan, 2016). As the professional team member who is explicitly tasked to examine the whole child in the context of home and community, it is essential for school social workers to foster a discussion about the impact of a child's trauma experiences as an important element of the assessment to tease out the driving forces behind school failure.

A confounding issue is that IDEA and the DSM are used primarily by different professions, have different purposes, and use different nomenclature.

IDEA uses an academic model that is designed for educators to determine eligibility for special education and related services under one of the disability categories. The DSM uses a medical model that is designed for mental health professionals as a diagnostic tool for psychiatric treatment and a payment system for public and private insurance payments.

For children who have experienced trauma, demonstration of learning readiness and school connection do not top the list of their interests. Instead safety, connection, and predicability are the driving forces, and, in desperation, their behaviors will demonstrate their fierce needs to secure these experiences, making eligibility decisions very difficult. The question is whether the evaluation data indicate that they qualify under IDEA for services under the category of "emotional disturbance" or whether material points to a DSM-5 disorder under the categories of disruptive, impulse control, and conduct disorders or neurodevelopmental disorders, formerly known as ADHD (Center for Behavioral Health Statistics and Quality, 2016). The answer makes a huge difference because a student with an emotional disturbance qualifies for special education, whereas a "socially maladjusted" student does not. The overlap between emotional problems and social maladjustment sometimes creates confusion because students display behaviors that are characteristic of both conditions. According to IDEA, in the final analysis, students determined to have an emotional disability along with social maladjustment are entitled to special education and related services. Legal opinions have suggested that there needs to be a new subcategory that identifies trauma as a classification for eligibility under the category of "emotional disturbance" for services (Winder, 2015).

Traumatic events have a big reach, and teasing out academic challenges grounded in emotional problems from noncompliant disruptive behavior problems is not a small piece of work. School social workers are in tune with the school culture and resources available for identified students. In some instances, school social workers can provide consultation to adults who interact with the child in the school setting, and help plan prevention services consistent with tier I and tier II, providing a stronger case for the need for special education if these plans do not achieve success. In other instances, schools have limited resources, leading you to push very hard for tier III or special education placement based on your knowledge of the child and the school setting. All these choices are important, leading to proper identification, placement, and implementation. It may take an entire academic year or more to arrive at an accurate determination, as described in Johnny's story presented in Box 3.2.

Box 3.2 Johnny's Story

Johnny is a nine-year old boy who arrived in Virginia four days before the start of the school year. He had been living with his grandmother in Honduras while his mother lived in the United States for the past six years. Johnny witnessed his father's murder two years ago, and he was already affiliated with a gang. His grandmother had difficulty managing his behavior while in Honduras. He took a dangerous journey to the United States by ground, during which he witnessed the rape of his female teenage guide. At the border, he was detained by ICE. He was placed in a safe house/group home for 6 weeks before his mother could arrange for reunification. He received therapy while in the group home, but he has not been in treatment since then.

Johnny enrolled in his neighborhood elementary school, where he was aggressive and defiant. He hit his teacher, refused to follow directions or participate in class, and had conflict with peers. Johnny was referred to the Local Special Education Screening Committee at his school because of these behaviors, as well as academic performance problems. The team did a full evaluation, and when they reconvened at the eligibility meeting, they went through the emotional disability criteria. At that time, the team felt they were unable to rule out social maladjustment, and he was found ineligible for special education. Soon after, Johnny had a significant issue with peers on the bus where he was violent, resulting in school suspension with the recommendation for expulsion. Johnny went through a disciplinary hearing and was placed in the county alternative school, rather than a program for students with emotional disabilities, because he was not found eligible as a special education student.

Johnny continued to have behavioral and academic problems at the alternative school and was referred a second time to the Special Education Screening Committee. In preparation for this new assessment, the school social worker collected more information about Johnny's past and current experiences from a trauma-informed perspective. The aim was to reframe the eligibility discussions so that some of Johnny's extreme difficulty in dealing appropriately with other people and his inability to cope in social situations might have its origins in a psychiatric disorder rather than a personality disorder.

To this end, the school social worker learned more about Johnny's trauma history over the course of a few months. He disclosed that while living in Honduras, he was required by the gang to carry a gun. He had been involved in a few shootings, and he was unsure whether he had killed people in Honduras. Johnny was trained to be hypervigilant. He reported this meant that he always on alert, and if loud noises occurred in school, he was often seen jumping from his chair and fearful.

Johnny's mother reported that now he gets upset easily. He is consistently aggressive in public and private settings—at the park, home, and school. Johnny is aggressive toward his younger siblings, hitting them, snatching items from them, and pushing them. The family currently rents a room in an apartment, and he has been stealing from the people who live in the apartment. His mother puts him to bed at 9 pm, but he won't stay in the bed. He pretends to sleep, but most times falls asleep around 2 am, which results in him getting approximately 4 to 6 hours of sleep per night. He broke a glass while in a car, and he intentionally took a piece of the glass and cut his finger. Johnny knows that his mother is dealing with her own health issues. She has cysts in her brain that require surgery. She will also be starting chemotherapy soon.

The school social worker also collected information about Johnny's strengths and resilience to include in the sociocultural evaluation. For example, she learned that Johnny was picked up by the police for hitchhiking. When questioned about this action, he reported that he missed the bus and was trying to get to school. In another instance, teachers became suspicious about a large amount of money that Johnny brought to school. It turned out that over the weekend he was out in his neighborhood when he saw a family loading up a moving van. He asked if they needed help. The family hired him for the day and paid him for his work.

Most important, the school social worker involved Johnny's mother so that she was an integral part of the assessment process. She has committed to following through with services and acknowledges that she needs the support. After more observation of Johnny, as well as meetings with community supports and his mother, the school social worker was able to advocate on his behalf that his aggressive, violent behavior in school was likely due to his trauma history and cultural experiences and that his needs fit the emotional disability criteria for special education.

Resources

Child Mind Institute. (2018). *Resources for educators.* Retrieved from https://childmind.org/audience/for-educators/

The Child Mind Institute is a national nonprofit dedicated to helping children who are struggling with behavioral, emotional, and learning difficulties. This webpage provides resources to help educators identify mental health and learning disorders accurately, as well as strategies to help make the learning environment better for everyone.

The National Child Traumatic Stress Network. (2016). *Is it ADHD or child traumatic stress: A guide for clinicians.* Los Angeles, CA & Durham, NC: National Center for Child Traumatic Stress. Retrieved from http://www.nctsn.org/sites/default/files/assets/pdfs/adhd_and_child_traumatic_stress_final.pdf

The National Child Traumatic Stress Network created a guide for clinicians to differentiate between symptoms of ADHD and childhood traumatic stress and areas of overlap. The guide provides tips for assessment and treatment.

References

Afifi, T. O., McMillan, K. A., Asmundson, G. J. G., Pietrzak, R. H., & Sareen, J. (2011). An examination of the relation between conduct disorder, childhood and adulthood traumatic events, and posttraumatic stress disorder in a nationally representative sample. *Journal of Psychiatric Research, 45,* 1564–1572.

American Psychiatric Association. (2013). *Diagnostic and statistical manual of mental disorders* (5th ed.). Washington, DC: Author.

Bagot, R. C., & Meaney, M. J. (2010). Epigenetics and the biological basis of gene x environmental interactions. *Journal of the American Academy of Child & Adolescent Psychiatry, 49*(8), 752–771.

Barnett, D. (2012). A grounded theory for identifying students with emotional disturbance: Promising practices for assessment, intervention, and service delivery. *Contemporary School Psychology: Formerly "The California School Psychologist," 16*(1), 21–31.

Beach, S. R. H., Brody, G. H., Lei, M. K., Gibbons, F. X., Gerrard, M., Simmons, R. L., . . . Cutrona, C. E. (2013). Impact of child sex abuse on adult psychopathology: A genetically and epigenetically informed investigation. *Journal of Family Psychology,* 27(1), 3–11.

Becker, K., Brandt, N., Stephan, S., & Chorpita, B. (2014). A review of educational outcomes in the children's mental health treatment literature. *Advances in School Mental Health Promotion,* 7(1), 5–23.

Bernhard, A., Martinelli, A., Ackerman, K., Saure, D., & Freitag, C. M. (2018). Association of trauma, posttraumatic stress disorder and conduct disorder: A systematic review and meta-analysis. *Neuroscience and Biobehavioral Reviews,* 91, 153–169.

Berthelot, N., Paccalet, T., Gilbert, E., Moreau, I., Mérette, C., Gingras, N., Rouleau, N., & Maziade, M. (2015). Childhood abuse and neglect may induce deficits in cognitive precursors of psychosis in high-risk children. *Journal of Psychiatry & Neuroscience,* 40(5), 336–343.

Biederman, J., Petty, C. R., Woodworth, K. Y., Bhide, P., Zhu, J., & Faraone, S. V. (2013). Examining the nature of the comorbidity between pediatric attention-deficit/hyperactivity disorder and posttraumatic stress disorder. *European Neuropsychopharmacology,* 23.

Brave Heart, M. Y. H., Chase, J., Elkins, J., & Altschul, D. B. (2011). Historical trauma among indigenous peoples of the Americas: Concepts, research, and clinical considerations. *Journal of Psychoactive Drugs,* 43(4), 282–290.

Center for Behavioral Health Statistics and Quality. (2016). *2014 National Survey on Drug Use and Health: DSM-5 changes: Implications for child serious emotional disturbance.* Substance Abuse and Mental Health Services Administration, Rockville, MD. Retrieved from https://www.samhsa.gov/data/sites/default/files/NSDUH-DSM5ImpactChildSED-2016.pdf

D'Andrea, W., Ford, J., Stolbach, B., Spinazzola, J., & van der Kolk, B. A. (2012). Understanding interpersonal trauma in children: Why we need a developmentally appropriate trauma diagnosis. *American Journal of Orthopsychiatry,* 82(2), 187–200.

Ehlers, C. L., Gizer, I. R., Gilder, D. A., Ellingson, J. M., & Yehuda, R. (2013). Measuring historical trauma in an American Indian community sample: Contributions of substance dependence, affective disorder, conduct disorder and PTSD. *Drug and Alcohol Dependence,* 133(1), 180–187.

Felitti, V. J., Anda, R. F., Nordenberg, D., Williamson, D. F., Spitz, A. M., Edwards, V., Koss, M. P., & Marks, J. S. (1998). Relationship of childhood abuse and household dysfunction to many of the leading causes of death in adults: The Adverse Childhood Experiences (ACE) study. *American Journal of Preventive Medicine,* 14, 245–258.

Gilliam, W. (2005). *Prekindergarteners left behind: Expulsion rates in state prekindergarten systems.* New Haven, CT: Yale University Child Study Center.

Gonzalez, A., Monzon, N., Solis, D., Jaycox, L., & Langley, A. K. (2016). Trauma exposure in elementary school children: Description of screening procedures, level of exposure, and posttraumatic stress symptoms. *School Mental Health,* 8, 77–88.

Grasso, D., Boonsiri, J., Lipschitz, D., Guyer, A., Houshyar, S., Douglas-Palumberi, H., . . . Kaufman, J. (2009). Posttraumatic stress disorder: The missed diagnosis. *Child Welfare,* 88(4), 157–176.

Harstad, E., & Levy S. (2014). Attention deficit/hyperactivity disorder and substance abuse. *American Academy of Pediatrics,* 134, 293–301.

Heinrich, A., Buchman, A., Zohsel, K., Dukal, H., Frank, J., Treutlein J., . . . Rietschel, M. (2015). Alterations of glucocorticoid receptor gene methylation in externalizing disorders during childhood and adolescence. *Behavioral Genetics, 45*(5), 529–536.

Henderson, Z., Acquaye-Doyle, L. A., Waites, S., & Howard, T. (2016). Putting principles into practice: Addressing historical trauma, mistrust, and apprehension in research methods courses. *Journal of Social Work Education, 52*(1), 69–78.

Holmes, C., Levy, M., Smith, A., Pinne, S., & Neese, P. (2015). A model for creating a supportive trauma-informed culture for children in preschool settings. *Journal of Child and Family Studies, 24,*1650–1659.

Holt, M. K., Finkelhor, D., & Kantor, G. K. (2007). Multiple victimization experience of urban elementary school students: Associations with psychosocial functioning and academic performance. *Child Abuse & Neglect, 31,* 503–515.

Individuals with Disabilities Education Improvement Act of 2004. 20 U.S.C. Section 1414.

Lamers-Winkelman, F., Willemen, A. A., & Visser, M. (2012). Adverse childhood experiences of referred children exposed to intimate partner violence: Consequences for their well-being. *Child Abuse and Neglect, 36*(2), 166–179.

Lester, B. M., Marsit, C. J., & Bromer, C. (2014). Behavioral epigenetics and the developmental origins of child mental health disorders. In K. Brandt, B. D. Perry, S. Seligman, & E. Troncik (Eds.), *Infant and early childhood mental health: Core concepts and clinical practice* (pp. 161–173).

Mehta, D., Klengel., T., Conneely, K. N., Smith, A. K., Altman, A., Pace, T. W., . . . Binder, E. B. (2013). Childhood maltreatment is associated with distinct genomic and epigenetic profiles in posttraumatic stress disorder. *PNAS Proceedings of the National Academy of Sciences of the United States of America, 110*(20), 8302–8307.

Mirabito, D., & Callahan, J. (2016). School-based trauma-informed care for traumatic events: Clinical and organizational practice. In C. R. Massat, M. S. Kelly, & R. Constable (Eds.), *School social work: Practice, policy, and research* (pp. 610–64). Chicago, IL; Lyceum Books, Inc.

Montalvo-Ortiz, J. L., Gelernter, J., Hudziak, J., & Kaufman, J. (2016). RDoC and translational perspectives on the genetics of trauma-related psychiatric disorders. *American Journal of Medical Genetics, 171*(1), 81–91.

National Child Traumatic Stress Network Schools Committee. (2008). *Child trauma toolkit for educators.* Los Angeles, CA & Durham, NC: National Center for Child Traumatic Stress.

Najavits, L. M., & Hein, D. (2013). Helping vulnerable populations: A comprehensive review of the treatment outcome literature on substance use disorder and PTSD. *Journal of Clinical Psychology, 69*(5), 433–479.

Nemeroff, C. B., & Binder, E. (2014). The preeminent role of childhood abuse and neglect in vulnerability to major psychiatric disorders. Toward elucidating the underlying neurobiological mechanisms. *Journal of the American Academy of Child & Adolescent Psychiatry, 53*(4), 395–397.

Nestler, E. J. (2016) Transgenerational epigenetic contributions to stress responses: Fact or fiction? *PLoS Biology, 14*(3), e1002426.

Norman, R. E., Byambaa, M., De, R., Butchart, A., Scott, J., & Vos, T. (2012). The long-term health consequences of child physical abuse, emotional abuse, and neglect: A systematic review and meta-analysis. *PLoS Medicine, 9*(11) doi:10.1371/journal.pmed.1001349

Nutton, J., & Fast, E. (2015). Historical trauma, substance use, and indigenous peoples: Seven generations of harm from a 'Big Event.' *Substance Use & Misuse, 50*(7), 839–847.

Oh, G., Wang, S-C., Pal, M., Chen, Z. F., Khare, T., Tochigi, M., . . . Patronis, A. (2015). DNA modification study of major depressive disorder: Beyond locus-by-locus comparisons. *Biological Psychiatry, 77*(3), 246–255.

Painter R. C., Roseboom T.J., & Bleker O. P. (2005). Prenatal exposure to the Dutch famine and disease in later life: An overview. *Reproductive Toxicology, 20*(3), 345–352.

Pariante, C. M. (2014). Depression during pregnancy: Molecular regulations of mothers' and children's behavior. *Biochemical Society Transactions, 42*(2), 582–586.

Perfect, M., Turley, M., Carlson, J., Yohanna, J., & Gilles, M. P. S. (2016). School-related outcomes of traumatic event exposure and traumatic stress symptoms in students: A systematic review of research from 1990–2015. *School Mental Health 8*, (1), 7–43.

Porche, M., Costello, D., & Rosen-Reynoso, M. (2016). Adverse family experiences, child mental health, and educational outcomes for a national sample of students. *School Mental Health 8*, (1), 44–60.

Raines, J. C. (2019). *Evidence-based practice in school mental health: Addressing DSM-5 disorders in schools.* New York, NY: Oxford University Press.

Sanderud, K., Murphy, S., & Elklit, A. (2016). Child maltreatment and ADHD symptoms in a sample of young adults. *European Journal of Psychotraumatology, 7*(1). doi:10.3402/ejpt.v7.32061

Sege, R. D., & Amaya-Jackson, L. (2017). Clinical considerations related to the behavioral manifestations of child maltreatment. *Pediatrics, 139*(4). doi:10.1542/peds.2017-0100.

Shin, S. H., Edwards, E. M., & Heeren, T. (2009). Child abuse and neglect: Relations to adolescent binge drinking in the national longitudinal study of adolescent health. *Addictive Behaviors, 34*(3), 277–280.

van der Kolk, B. A., & Courtois, C. (2005). Editorial comments: Complex developmental trauma. *Journal of Traumatic Stress, 18*(5), 385–388.

Winder, F. (2015). Childhood trauma and special education: Why the "IDEA" is failing today's impacted youth. *Hofstra Law Review, 44*(2), 601–634.

Wong, C. C. Y., Meaburn, E. L., Ronald, A., Price, T. S., Jeffries, A. R. Schalkwyk, L. C., . . . Mill, J. (2014). Methylomic analysis of monozygotic twins discordant for autism spectrum disorder and related behavioural traits. *Molecular Psychiatry, 19*(4), 495–503.

Zarate-Garza, P. P., Biggs, B. K., Croarkin, P., Morath, B., Leffler, J., Cuellar-Barboza, A., & Tye, S. J. (2017). How well do we understand the long-term health implications of childhood bullying? *Harvard Review of Psychiatry, 25*(2), 89–95.

4

■ ■ ■

Creating Safe Environments for Traumatized Children in Schools

The Three Pillars of Trauma Care in Schools

As outlined in Chapters 2 and 3, exposure to traumatic events in childhood and adolescence can have lasting negative social, emotional, and educational effects. For schools, or any environment that serves children, to be truly trauma-informed, they must address three crucial areas: safety, connection, and emotional and behavioral regulation. This chapter will explore these three areas as the foundational pillars of a trauma-informed structure. Each area will be explored, along with examples of how they can be created in a school environment.

Safety

At their core, all traumatic events are a violation of a sense of safety in the world and with others. People and places that are supposed to be attuned to the needs of children are often the ones that violate trust through abuse, neglect, and violence. Given that the caregiver-child relationship is the foundation on which the child's senses of safety, competence, and self-containment are built, when this relationship is strife with traumatic events, those capacities are severely compromised (Arvidson et al., 2011). Abusive parents and caregivers, violence in communities, and shootings in schools are all too commonplace in American culture. The presence of traumatic stress has long-lasting negative impacts on children, and when severe and prolonged, it can be so toxic that it leads to neurological and biological health problems (Walkley & Cox, 2013).

What does safety look like? For children and adolescents, safety is felt through connections with people who have a calm and focused presence. They are attuned to the child's actions, words, and nonverbal communications and respect their boundaries and rights. Power and control are essential to safety in that the child is allowed to be in charge of himself or herself as much as is developmentally appropriate. When power is used to be punitive and demeaning, children do not feel safe. When seeking safety, children look for someone to be predictable and consistent. Following through on what they say they are going to do and avoiding chaotic and disorganized behaviors are essential to safety. All these require the person to stay calm, regulated, and focused when the child is dysregulated, out of control, or even aggressive. Some examples of safe and unsafe behaviors in a school setting are found in Box 4.1.

Classrooms that feel safe to children are those that have clear expectations, well-defined routines, time for transition, choices whenever possible, and attuned teachers. Specific events in the classroom can serve as reminders of previous traumatic and therefore unsafe experiences. These current events *trigger* reminders of past events (Pickens & Tschopp, 2017). Some examples of triggers in a classroom setting that can prompt a child to react from a place of traumatic stress and feeling unsafe are:

- Sensory reminders of the trauma—smells, sounds, or images that remind the child of a person, place, or time that is connected to a traumatic event.
- Touch—whether to focus the child with a gentle hand on the shoulder or a physical restraint of a child who is a danger to others. Touch that is unwanted or unexpected can be a trauma trigger.
- Fighting, arguing, or yelling, whether between children or between an adult and a child.

These can be difficult for teachers to anticipate and manage because one cannot predict what a trigger might be for a specific child, while other triggers can be managed by decreasing behavior such as yelling by the teacher or adult in charge. For example, a child may have a traumatic stress reaction when triggered by the smell of an orange. Perhaps that child was abused by a caregiver who regularly ate oranges and the smell of the orange being peeled reminds the child of that person and the abusive behavior.

Box 4.1 Safe and Unsafe Behaviors

Safe	Unsafe
Focusing on the student when they speak to you.	Not making eye contact, looking away or at something else when the student is speaking.
Speaking in a moderated tone and volume.	Yelling, muttering under your breath, or whispering to someone else.
Consistent behavior so that the student knows what to expect when he or she encounters you.	Erratic, unpredictable behavior.
Clear rules that apply to everyone, with consequences appropriate to the violation.	No rules, rules that are randomly and unevenly applied, or punitive measures that do not match the rule violation.
Ability to control emotions and stay calm.	Big emotional swings or outbursts; easily startled or rattled.
Boundaries are communicated; others' boundaries are respected.	No boundaries are set, and others' boundaries are not followed.
Attention and care for all students.	Some students are clear favorites who get preferential treatment.
Students are allowed privacy in the bathroom and are allowed to leave the classroom to go to a safe place if they feel triggered and unsafe.	Threats are used to keep the student feeling unable to leave the classroom for any reason.
Unconditional, positive regard for all students.	Some students are judged for their behavior, and their behavior is taken personally.
Honesty and transparency.	Lying, obfuscating, or refusing to explain reasons for actions.
All students are held to high standards and expected to work to their ability.	Ignoring or not expecting much from some students because of their "problems."

A teacher would have no way of anticipating this, and the child may not even be aware that the smell of the orange is a trigger until that moment when the child is emotionally reactive, out of control, or dissociative. What teachers can do is be curious about what may have prompted the sudden change in that child and include a traumatic trigger as one of the possible explanations for the behavior. They also may pick up clues to triggering events by listening carefully to the way children discuss subjective experiences. There are signs about how a child primarily receives, interprets, and transmits sensory stimuli and expresses them in terms of sight (visual), sound (auditory), touch (kinesthetic), smell (olfactory), and taste (gustatory) (Angell, 2017). Does a child use representational language that *pictures, hears, feels, whiffs,* or *flavors* an experience that may be helpful in recognizing how a child is triggered? Trauma-informed practices mean being compassionate and seeing behaviors and actions as attempts to express distress and seek safety (Wolpow, Johnson, Hertel, & Kincaid, 2016). Current events provide ample evidence of how important it is to understand the impact of violence on child development and learning. Box 4.2 makes an important point for school social workers to advocate for an educational plan in response to events that are considered the purview of civil or criminal authorities.

Connection

Children who have had traumatic experiences inflicted on them by adults learn that adults are not to be trusted. Children entering a new school or a new classroom will be careful around adults and will watch closely for indications that they need to protect themselves. This sense of hypervigilance and wariness will make it difficult for them to connect with adults in a school setting, but connection is essential for the development of safe, trauma-informed settings (Bath, 2008). Power imbalances also disrupt connection. In the classroom, teachers are in charge and make the rules, which can lead children to feel powerless. If a child has experienced an adult using his or her power to abuse others, this power imbalance will impair connection. It may also create a situation in which the child seeks power and control to feel safe, which creates disconnection (Wolpow, Johnson, Hertel, & Kincaid, 2016). In trauma-informed classrooms, teachers recognize this dynamic and strive to create corrective experiences with an adult who is associated with positive experiences. Trauma can be re-enacted in relationships with adults who react

School violence and crisis preparedness were brought into sharp relief in 2018 at the *March for Our Lives* when hundreds of thousands of people gathered on the Mall in Washington, DC, after the school massacre in Parkland, Florida. Yet, research and scholarship vary on ways to prevent school violence and develop school crisis, emergency management, and medical response plans (Benbenishty & Astor, 2005; Cornell, Allen, & Fan, 2012; Miller, Martin, & Schamess, 2003).

It is incumbent on school social workers involved in trauma-informed schools to remember that school safety is an *educational issue* (Klinger, 2018) because it is viewed often as a law enforcement issue. Policymakers, police, emergency services, and health and mental health professionals approach school safety from their own perspectives. The real questions are what safety measures make sense for *students* and what is an appropriate plan based on their *age and developmental needs*? The best safety and security plans for a school are not the same as those for a shopping mall!

To strengthen trauma-informed practices, school social workers must facilitate *dialogue* to create a comprehensive approach that addresses multiple hazards, not just an active shooter scenario. Injury and death from suicide, car accidents, medical illness, or sports injury upend students' sense of well-being just as much as gun violence. Legislative mandates and district policies do not equate to a broad, deep, and rich discussion between community stakeholders and among all school personnel. School social workers are well qualified to develop these discussions given our professional training on the stressors engendered by faulty transactions between individuals and their environments.

to the child's search for safety, power, and control with anger, punishment, suspicion, and distance (van der Kolk, 2005).

In a school setting, most adults are there to help children learn and grow. However, adults can get drawn into a trauma re-enactment with a child who is testing them to learn how they respond. Often, this is not done purposefully but instead comes from a defensive, self-protective action when a child engages as he or she would with the abusive adult. In other words, in order to know what to expect and to confirm the child's suspicion that the adult is unsafe, the child may engage in a conflictual way. This can be done through behavior that is aggressive or unsafe, verbal assaults designed to hurt or bring about rejection, or mistreatment of another child in the classroom. This child will often be described as being "provocative" or "self-sabotaging," but it is important to not label but rather to wonder why. Why would this child behave this way? When this is seen as a traumatic reaction, a self-protection against vulnerability and being harmed yet again by an adult the child is are supposed to be able to trust, it makes sense. It is a survival behavior. When viewed in this manner, it can be helpful in not personalizing the behavior. When the adult does not respond as expected, then there is hope for safety.

In order to establish connection in school settings, it can be helpful to start off the school year by setting some ground rules for the classroom and asking each student to voice his or her own needs, either by creating a rule or agreeing with a rule made by a peer. Connecting with each student's basic need for safety and respect is a good start. Connecting to children through their behavior is also a way to get to know them better (Craig, 2008; Souers & Hall, 2016). Instead of responding in anger or exasperation to a student who is "acting out," respond with curiosity. "I noticed that you threw your pen across the room when I corrected your spelling. I'm wondering if you noticed that too, and what you think that's about?" This neutral, curious, and concerned stance shows the child that you are not judging but want to connect.

The school environment offers a major opportunity for children to develop positive experiences through new social interactions with adults and peers that are in contrast to their own negative models of relationship. Classroom connections for maltreated students are developed through consistent adult responses, helping them to understand the rules that create predictable responses. Peer interactions are the hallmark of school-aged children's experiences, and classrooms are a natural context within which to help traumatized children make classmate connections (Astor & Benbenishty, 2018).

Routines and rituals are an antidote to life's chaos and disruptions, allowing children to shift out of survival mode and into new patterns of adaptive social interactions with adults (Blaustein & Kinniburgh, 2010). Rather than reacting to overt behaviors, teachers can model for students how to react to the emotional message behind a student's behavior. They can help children learn strategies for negotiating interpersonal problems in a supportive context. Research shows that children flourish when they can predict environmental responses and understand the rules for interactions (Blaustein & Kinniburgh, 2010).

Regulation

The ability to appropriately manage feelings, emotions, and impulses is impaired by childhood trauma (Kinniburgh, Blaustein, Spinazzola, & van der Kolk, 2005). Emotional arousal can feel scary to a child who has not been taught how to self-soothe and calm down. Imagine you are hearing an alarm go off in your house; it's loud, dark, and scary, and you cannot find where the noise is coming from to turn it off. In these cases children need to be taught how to identify and appropriately express emotions. They also require guidance on how to tolerate distressing emotions and calm themselves through self-soothing and self-regulation (Kinniburgh, Blaustein, Spinazzola, & van der Kolk, 2005). In a classroom setting, adults can help children with this essential task in a number of ways:

1. Label the emotions you see the children demonstrating. This will give them the language they are lacking. Much like learning the Spanish word for "door," the children are learning the language of emotions. By labeling the emotion as it is being expressed, the children learn what is going on inside themselves and also are calmed by that knowledge (Lieberman et al., 2011).
2. Place emotion faces with the identifying labels around the classroom. This will help children develop the language of emotion as they learn what sad, happy, confused, and so forth look like.
3. Provide an opportunity to reflect on the behavior and feelings exhibited (Wolpow et al., 2016). Depending on the developmental stage, this can take the form of a drawing, poem, or essay. Having a quiet space in the school where the child can go to reflect and process what happened and why is a wonderful way to achieve this task.
4. Work with the child to calm down. This is also known as co-regulation and is particularly useful with adolescents (Bath, 2008b). By focusing on the emotions, not the behaviors, and staying calm while speaking in a soothing voice, the adult identifies the distress and invites the child into a reflective, problem-solving encounter.

5. Add calming and mindfulness exercises for all the kids in the class during times of transition. This can be particularly good after a test or a fire/safety drill. These exercises can include listening to breathing, lying on the floor with a stuffed animal on the stomach and watching it move up and down (Wolpow et al., 2016), mindfully eating a small piece of chocolate or candy while focusing on the taste and sensations in their bodies, or other activities.

6. Use times of emotional dysregulation and distress as an opportunity to educate children about how their brain works and how we can all get overwhelmed by feelings. Neuroscientist Dan Siegel has great videos on his website that explain how the brain works (drdansiegel.com). These videos can be shown to individual kids or to the entire class to help them better understand some of the brain science behind behaviors.

Box 4.3, Fear, Disconnection, and Dysregulation, offers a resource for school social workers to use in educating children, families, and educators about the

---

Box 4.3 Fear, Disconnection, and Dysregulation

Adults in the school setting actually have a lot of control in developing a sense of safety, connection, and regulation for *all* students. Setting aside a small amount of time to create plans and letting students have the opportunity to participate in the development of the classroom culture can positively affect the remaining classroom time. Rather than trying to control behavior, the aim is to work toward eliminating a sense of threat and unpredictability by utilizing daily routines and a nonjudgmental tone of voice and becoming aware of one's own triggers and how to manage them (Bailey, 2018).

How to Create a Bully is an excellent explanation of the connection between regulation problems and problems in the home, school, and community. It explores each developmental stage and the warning signs for negative school behaviors. It identifies crucial crossroads in the child's life where school social workers can intervene to prevent aggression toward self and others due to fear, disconnection, and dysregulation. To access the video, visit https://www.youtube.com/watch?v=tzftHNh7xP8.

---

connection between bullying and maladaptive behaviors across the child development spectrum and in school settings. An example of what this would look like with a child struggling in school can be found Ethan's Story in Box 4.4, along with Skill Box 4.1, which provides more information on the Take Five Breathing technique described in the case.

Box 4.4 Ethan's Story

Trauma Type: Currently homeless, witness to domestic violence, limited contact with strong attachment figure, bullying
Culture/Ethnicity: Filipino

Presenting Problem

Ethan is an eight-year-old, Filipino boy who is currently in third grade at a local elementary school. Ethan and his family have been homeless for several months. Ethan, his mother, his mother's boyfriend, and his grandmother are living in a local family shelter. According to assessment data, Ethan reports having witnessed domestic violence at home and reports being bullied at school. Ethan uses humor to engage peers, which causes disruption in the classroom and has initiated fights among students. Ethan demonstrates multiple signs of arousal, including difficulty sleeping, impaired concentration, hypervigilance, and increased startle response. Ethan is connected with the mental health team at his school for services.

Background/History

Ethan currently lives with his mother, mother's boyfriend, and grandmother at a local family shelter. Ethan and his family have been homeless for several months. Ethan's father moved to a different state when Ethan was three years old and has three young children. Ethan has limited contact with his father and half-siblings. Ethan has witnessed significant domestic and community violence throughout his childhood. Ethan was enrolled in a different elementary school

---

Creating Trauma-Informed Schools

last year because of his living situation, so this is his first year at this elementary school. Ethan has been connected with the mental health team since entering school to address his emotional and behavioral issues.

Reason for Referral

Ethan has consistently struggled in elementary school, as evidenced by his poor concentration, use of humor to engage classmates during class, difficulty with redirection, and frequent altercations with other students. Ethan is currently receiving services from his elementary school's mental health team but was referred to the Trauma Focused Cognitive Behavioral Therapy (TF-CBT) groups offered by an outside agency for additional support. The application of the three pillars of trauma care in schools has been critical to Ethan's success in the group. Ethan attends the weekly TF-CBT group and has learned and practiced emotion regulation skills and relaxation techniques to help manage his emotions. Through repeated exposure and practice of feeling identification, Ethan has been better able to communicate his feelings and needs instead of using alternative coping skills, such as humor or teasing. The consistency and safety of the space, which clinicians strive to keep consistent week to week, is essential for helping Ethan transition into the space and staying regulated while in group. Ethan has responded well to redirection during group and uses his emotion regulation skills, such as Take Five Breathing, to help regulate his emotions and behavior. Ethan is able to use Take Five Breathing independently when he notices he needs to slow down and also responds well when prompted by the clinician to "Take Five." The connection that is also fostered between clinicians and group members has also contributed to making the space safe and accepting. Through participation in the TF-CBT group founded in the pillars of safety, connection, and managing emotions, Ethan has had fewer behavioral issues at school, as evidenced by a decrease in instances of being sent to the principal's office and taken out of a class.

Skill Box 4.1 Take Five Breathing

Take Five Breathing, also known as rollercoaster breathing, can be used in any setting and with children of all ages. The purpose of Take Five Breathing is to help an activated child slow down and regain focus. Once a child practices Take Five Breathing a few times, it can be used as an easy prompt when you notice that a child is becoming increasingly activated. To start, stick out one hand in front of you and spread the fingers wide apart, like a star. Using your index finger of your other hand, start at the outside base of the thumb and breathe in slowly through the nose as the finger moves up to the top of the thumb. Direct the child to pause briefly at the top of the thumb and then breathe out slowly through the mouth as the finger traces the inside of the thumb. Continue breathing in on the "up" movements and breathing out on the "down" movements. As the child is tracing each finger, prompt the child to focus on his or her breath as well as what the small movements on their hand feel like. In addition to slowing down breathing, this will also create more mind-body awareness. If a child needs more time to regulate, encourage the child to continue repeating the exercise as many times as needed.

Through establishing safety, connection, and regulation in schools, the three pillars create the foundation of a trauma-informed structure for children in schools. The more children feel safe and connected to the adults around them, the more they can learn to understand and regulate their emotions and behaviors. This creates a safe learning environment for all children. The School Social Work Association of America has taken a stand on this issue. Box 4.5 provides their statement.

Just as cancer, motor vehicle collisions, and substance misuse are public health issues, so too is gun violence in American schools. Multiple-victim school shootings are both tragic and preventable. According to the American Public Health Association (2017), gun violence has become an epidemic, causing more than 30,000 deaths per year and 60,000 injuries with an average of nearly two dozen children killed every day. These deaths and injuries are especially grievous when they happen to our children within the supposed safety of their schools (Cox & Rich, 2018).

US Federal Bureau of Investigation (2017) data show that schools have become the second most common location for active shooting incidents from 2000 to 2016, with 22% occurring in education facilities. Indeed, some of the worst mass casualty shootings have occurred in our nation's schools, including Columbine (1999) with 13 victims, Red Lake, MN (2005) with 10 victims, Virginia Tech (2007) with 32 victims, Newtown, CT (2012) with 27 victims, and Parkland, FL (2018) with 17 victims.

A UN survey of 14 developed nations found that all require gun licensing and all but one have gun storage laws, while the United States has neither. American children, ages 5 to 14, are 13 times more likely to be murdered with a gun than children in other developed countries, and 85% of all children murdered in the 14 developed countries are American children (Newbergh, 2013). According to research, guns have become the third most common cause of death for children in America (Fowler et al., 2017). While the School Social Work Association of America (SSWAA) acknowledges the Second Amendment right of individual citizens to keep and bear arms (District of Columbia v. Heller, 554 U.S. 570, 2008; McDonald v. Chicago, 561 U.S. 742, 2010), it also asserts that there are some commonsense ways to improve school safety and the right of our youngest citizens to possess the most basic of all human rights—the right to life (Raines, 2018). Accordingly, SSWAA:

1. Joins the American Academy of Pediatrics, the American Academy of Child & Adolescent Psychiatry, and the National Child Abuse Coalition (2015) in their recommendation that

Congress resume funding for the Centers for Disease Control and Prevention (CDC) to conduct research on the prevention of gun violence, especially in our nation's schools.

2. Supports gun policies that require criminal background checks for all firearms purchases, including those made at gun shows and on the Internet. Currently unlicensed private firearms sellers are exempt from conducting criminal background checks on buyers at gun shows or over the Internet, giving felons, the mentally ill, and others prohibited from owning firearms access to weapons.

3. Encourages expanded access to mental health services. Funding for mental health services has been declining, and funding for the Substance Abuse and Mental Health Services Administration continues to be threatened by budget cuts including cuts due to sequestration. We must ensure that state, local, and community-based behavioral health systems have the resources they need to provide much-needed care.

4. Supports resources for school-based violence prevention programs. In accordance with the Every Student Succeeds Act, we support the creation of positive behavior interventions and supports and early intervention strategies. These should include school-wide programs that address bullying, violence, anger management, and other social and emotional issues that impede academic achievement. We also support school-based mental health services, especially school social workers, to ensure that children and youths can access appropriate treatment and services (Cowan, Vaillancourt, Rossen, & Pollitt, 2013).

5. Supports appropriate security measures such as appointment of a safety ombudsman, securing entrances to the school and remote monitoring systems, installing a centralized security system linked to a local emergency response team and a centralized communication system within the school building, issuing identification badges to staff and students, guiding visitors through a sign-in process, and requiring parking permits for all cars parked on school property (Advancement Project, 2013).

6. Supports crisis planning in schools with thorough preparation for an emergency; a detailed communications strategy; school and neighborhood site maps; drills and trainings; a response plan to evacuate, reverse evacuate, lockdown, or shelter in place; and a plan for helping students and staff to recover from psychological trauma.

7. Supports more research into gun safety technology (Newbergh, 2013). Smart guns or personalized guns are firearms that includes safety features that only allow it to fire when activated by an authorized user. Such features may include the use of radiofrequency identification (RFID) chips, fingerprint recognition, magnetic rings, or mechanical locks. Using wide area control technology, weapons could be remotely disabled using wireless protocols so that safe zones could be created around schools.

8. Opposes placing more police, security guards, or resource officers in schools because (1) they have not been proved to make schools safer, (2) the resources could be used to support programs and safety alternatives that do work, and (3) they further exacerbate the criminalization of children, particularly for students of color and students with disabilities who are disproportionately disciplined and arrested in school (Advancement Project, 2013).

9. Opposes concealed carry options for school educators. As specialized instructional support personnel, SSWAA joins both the American Federation of Teachers and the National Education Association in stating that educators do not want to be feared as armed guards but do want to focus on our instructional roles in supporting sustainable school safety (Mroka & Busser, 2012).

10. If Congress refuses to reinstate the ban on semiautomatic assault weapons, SSWAA supports a requirement that the owners of such weapons be required to carry liability insurance in case the weapon is used against innocent civilians in order to compensate victims (or their families) for medical and funeral expenses incurred.

Resources

Conscious Discipline Model for Building Resilient Classrooms. (2018). Retrieved from consciousdisclipine.com

The Substance Abuse and Mental Health Services Administration (SAMHSA) and the National Registry of Evidence-based Programs and Practices (NREPP) have determined that conscious discipline is an evidence-based, trauma-informed approach for addressing student achievement and behaviors as well as school climate. Decreased discipline referrals, increased academic achievement, improved school culture, and healthier social and emotional skills sets are some of the key outcomes found for this model.

The website provides a wealth of information for teachers, administrators, mental health professionals, and parents, including free resources and video examples, that dig deeper into many of the principles and practices described in this book. It maps out how to transition from a traditional compliance discipline model to a conscious discipline school model. Integrating social-emotional learning principles, school culture, and discipline, it is a comprehensive program on how to work effectively with children who become reactive as a result of stress and trauma. It is designed to build a system of connections with students rather than a set of rewards and punishment, placing emphasis on internal self-regulation instead of external controls. Problem-solving is emphasized as a successful alternative to obedience.

The framework is built around the concepts of safety, connection, and problem-solving based on brain neurobiology scholarship and research. Children in a "survival state," or the most primitive level of brain functioning, are found to be soothed when a safe space is created for them. In an "emotional state," children benefit from their sense of connection and belonging. The executive state, the optimal level of functioning, sets the stage for students who feel safe and connected to exercise problem-solving skills that integrates learning experiences in different school situations.

In tandem with these concepts is the belief that adults need to concurrently work toward regulating their own actions in stressful situations, modeling the seven skills of composure, encouragement, assertiveness, choice, empathy, positive intent, and consequences. To develop these skills, "seven powers for conscious adults" are identified, along with the principle and goal behind each one, for developing greater emotional intelligence and new, effective patterns of responses in the face of antagonism, disorder, and chaos.

The Educator's School Safety Network. (2018). Retrieved from http://eschoolsafety.org

The Educator's School Safety Network is a national nonprofit organization that compiles academic research and provides training, consultation, and resources for educators and school systems to help keep students safe. Training covers important components of school safety, including school lockdown, threat assessment management, bomb incident management, parent reunification planning, improving practices for diverse students, and bus safety as part of an all-hazard approach to safe and supportive learning environments. A resource index and podcasts provide videos and live links on active shooter responses, bullying and cyberbullying, emergency operations planning, family emergency plans, LGBTQ resources, and school-based law enforcement. Recommendations for ensuring school safety through preparation, prevention, and responses are included.

Youth Violence Project. (2018). Retrieved from https://curry.virginia.edu/uploads/resourceLibrary/Virginia_Model_for_Student_Threat_Assessment_overview_paper_7-16-10.pdf

The "Model for Youth Threat Assessment" guide created by the Curry School of Education at the University of Virginia presents research and facts about youth violence and school safety. It discusses the development of threat assessment teams in schools and identifies seven steps that teams can take to develop a comprehensive model of school safety.

References

Advancement Project. (2013). *A real fix: The gun-free way to school safety.* Retrieved from https://b.3cdn.net/advancement/78db1dd92e7fc2f6e8_21m6bck09.pdf

American Academy of Pediatrics. (2015). *Letter in support of gun violence prevention research funding from health groups to Appropriations Committee.* Retrieved from http://www.phi.org/resources/?resource=letter-in-support-of-gun-violence-prevention-research-funding-from-health-groups-to-appropriations-committee-december-2015

American Public Health Association. (2017). *Preventing gun violence: Fact sheet.* Retrieved from https://www.apha.org/~/media/files/pdf/factsheets/160317_gunviolencefs.ashx

Angell, G. B. (2017). Neurolinguistic programming theory and social work treatment. In F. J. Turner (Ed.), *Social work treatment: Interlocking theoretical treatment* (6th ed., pp. 351–375). New York, NY: Oxford University Press.

Arvidson, J., Kinniburgh, K., Howard, K., Spinazzola, J., Strothers, H., Evans, M., Andres, B., Cohen, C., & Blaustein, M. E. (2011). Treatment of complex trauma in young children: Developmental and cultural considerations in application of the ARC intervention model. *Journal of Child & Adolescent Trauma, 4,* 34–51.

Astor, R. A., & Benbenishty R. (2018). *Mapping and monitoring bullying and violence: Building a safe school climate.* New York, NY: Oxford University Press.

Bailey, B. (2018). *Conscious discipline: Book portal, chapter 4: Composure.* Retrieved from https://consciousdiscipline.com/free-resources/book-portal/chapter-4-composure/

Bath, H. (2008). The three pillars of trauma-informed care. *Reclaiming Children and Youth, 17*(3), 17–21.

Bath, H. I. (2008b). Calming together: The pathway to self-control. *Reclaiming Children and Youth, 16*(4), 44–46.

Benbenishty, R., & Astor, R. (2005). *School violence in context: Culture, neighborhood, family, school and gender.* New York, NY: Oxford University Press.

Blaustein, M. E., & Kinniburgh, K. M. (2010). *Treating traumatic stress in children and adolescents: How to foster resilience through attachment, self-regulation, and competency.* New York, NY: The Guilford Press.

Cornell, D., Allen, K., & Fan, X. (2012). A randomized controlled study of the Virginia Student Threat Assessment Guidelines in grades K–12. *School Psychology Review, 41,* 100–115.

Cowan, K. C., Vaillancourt, K., Rossen, E., & Pollitt, K. (2013). *A framework for safe and successful schools [Brief].* Bethesda, MD: National Association of School Psychologists.

Cox, J. W., & Rich, S. (2018, February 15). No, there haven't been 18 school shootings in 2018. *Washington Post.* Retrieved from https://www.washingtonpost.com/local/no-there-havent-been-18-school-shooting-in-2018-that-number-is-flat-wrong/2018/02/15/65b6cf72-1264-11e8- 8ea1-c1d91fcec3fe_story.html?utm_term=.30a89f6c4f1f

Craig, S. E. (2008). *Reaching and teaching children who hurt: Strategies for your classroom.* Baltimore, MD: Brookes Publishing.

Fowler, K. A., Dahlberg, L. L., Haileyesus, T., Gutierrez, C., & Bacon, S. (2017). Childhood firearm injuries in the United States. *Pediatrics, 140*(1): e20163486. Retrieved from http://pediatrics.aappublications.org/content/early/2017/06/15/peds.2016-3486

Kinniburgh, K. J., Blaustein, M., Spinazzola, J., & van der Kolk, B. A. (2005). Attachment, self-regulation, and competency: A comprehensive intervention framework for children with complex trauma. *Psychiatric Annals, 35*(5), 424–430.

Klinger, A. (2018). *Empower, not intimidate: Emerging issues in school safety.* School Social Work Association of America, Violence Prevention Resources. Retrieved from https://www.sswaa.org/violence-prevention-resources

Lieberman, M. D., Inagaki, T. K., Tabibnia, G., & Crockett, M. J. (2011). Subjective responses to emotional stimuli during labeling, reappraisal, and distraction. *Emotion, 11*(3), 468–480.

Miller, J., Marten, I. R., & Schamess, G. (2003). *School violence and children in crisis: Community and school interventions for social workers and counselors.* Denver, CO: Love Publishing Co.

Mrowka, M., & Busser, C. (December 20, 2012). *AFT, NEA: Arming educators won't keep schools safe, focus needs to be on investments in mental health services, reasonable gun safety legislation.* Retrieved from http://www.nea.org/home/53943.htm

Newbergh, C. (2013, July 15). *Gun violence is "a problem we don't need to have"—The public health approach.* Retrieved from http://www.phi.org/news-events/503/gun-violence-is-a-problem- we-dont-need-to-have-the-public-health-approach

Pickens, I. B., & Tschopp, N. (2017). *Trauma-informed classrooms.* Reno, NV: The National Council of Juvenile and Family Court Judges.

Raines, J. C. (2018). *A public health approach to school safety & violence prevention.* London, KY: School Social Work Association of America.

Souers, K., & Hall, P. (2016). *Fostering resilient learners: Strategies for creating a trauma-sensitive classroom.* Alexandria, VA: ASCD Publishers.

US Federal Bureau of Investigation. (2017). *Quick look: 220 active shooter incidents in the United States between 2000–2016.* Retrieved from https://www.fbi.gov/about/partnerships/office-of- partner-engagement/active-shooter-incidents-graphics

van der Kolk, B. A. (2005) Developmental trauma disorder: Toward a rational diagnosis for children with complex trauma histories. *Psychiatric Annals, 35*(5), 401–408.

Walkley, M., & Cox, T. L. (2013). Building trauma-informed schools and communities. *Children & Schools, 35*(2), 123–126.

Wolpow, R., Johnson, M. M., Hertel, R., & Kincaid, S. O. (2016). *The heart of learning and teaching: Compassion, resiliency, and academic success* (3rd ed.). Retrieved from http://www.k12.wa.us/compassionateschools/pubdocs/TheHeartofLearningandTeaching.pdf

5

The Ten Principles of Trauma-Informed Services and Application to School Environments

Given that children spend a large portion of their day in school settings and that an estimated upward of 70% of children have experienced some form of trauma (Saunders & Adams, 2014), it behooves educators and school social workers to strive to create systems that attend to the dynamics presented by trauma, minimize traumatic reminders (triggers), and prevent revictimization. For a school to be considered trauma-informed, the services and care must be provided in the context of an organization-wide approach grounded in an understanding of trauma and its consequences, with a focus on strengths, healing, and resilience. This requires a shift in the questions that are asked about children who have trouble learning or who interrupt the learning of others. Instead of asking a child, "what's wrong with you?" the question becomes, "what happened to you?" Research shows that children who experience trauma are more likely to have behavioral and academic problems (Holmes et al., 2015); therefore, school settings must be equipped to meet these children where they are and to help them see school as a safe place. In the previous chapter, we explored the three pillars of trauma care in schools: safety, connection, and managing emotions. This chapter continues that focus by delving into ways in which school social workers can create trauma-informed environments in educational settings.

Social work practitioners and researchers generally agree on ten principles of trauma-informed services (Elliott et al., 2005). Each principle will be explored in depth with examples of how to apply each in a school setting. An 11th principle, care of the worker, will be added to help school social workers address vicarious trauma. Vicarious trauma is considered a natural byproduct of working with traumatized populations, and organizations have an obligation to support their workers within this context (Dombo & Blome, 2016; Dombo & Gray, 2013). The ten principles (Elliott et al., 2005) guide organizations to:

- Recognize the impact of trauma on development and coping behaviors
- Place recovery from trauma as a primary goal
- Use an empowerment model
- Maximizes the individual's control over the recovery process
- Use relational collaboration
- Address the need for safety, acceptance, and respect
- Focus on adaptation and resilience in a strengths-based manner
- Minimize the potential for more traumatic experiences
- Strive for cultural competence
- Involve consumers in program design and evaluation

Each principle will be explored in more detail with regard to school environments and the role of the school social worker.

Principle 1: Trauma-Informed Services Recognize the Impact of Violence and Victimization on Development and Coping Strategies

The very first principle requires educators and school social workers to learn about the developmental impact of trauma on children and to see behaviors as coping strategies. Schools can use professional development days for teachers to gain the knowledge, skills, and confidence necessary to identify and work with children who have trauma histories. The experience of trauma is seen as something that was done to the child, so the coping behaviors are understood through that lens, not as mental health pathology. For example, a child who is overwhelmed by emotions and has difficulty concentrating in class should not be automatically labeled as "explosive" or "inattentive." This child should be directed toward services in the school that allow him or her to express feelings through talk or expressive therapies and given skills to focus in the classroom setting. Family members should be made aware of the problems in the classroom, and resources for family work should also be provided. When approached in this manner, the school staff see the root cause of the barriers to learning as potentially caused by traumatic experiences the child has endured, not the child himself or herself.

Principle 2: Trauma-Informed Services Identify Recovery from Trauma as Primary Goal

While the primary focus for schools is education, not mental health, being a trauma-informed school means connecting the sequelae of trauma to barriers in learning. Therefore, if the primary goal is education, and a child who has a trauma history has difficulty learning, then healing from trauma becomes an important step on the learning journey. Programs either integrate trauma recovery into all services or offer specialized trauma services to clients (Elliott et al., 2005). Because integration is preferred, schools could consider addressing trauma symptoms in all aspects of the school environment. For example, the school nurse would screen for trauma history when a child comes to her office complaining of stomachache because she knows that trauma symptoms can be somatic. Education about coping with stress could be given by the nurse. Teachers could consider specific disciplinary action and its potential to be retraumatizing and create alternate behavioral intervention strategies. In all these efforts, healing from trauma would be viewed as a priority for schools in an effort to ensure that all children are able to learn.

Principle 3: Trauma-Informed Services Employ an Empowerment Model

Children who experience trauma have been powerless. Schools can contribute to the empowerment of all children by placing the children in charge of themselves. School social workers provide the conduit between the children and their learning environment, which means they are a powerful ally in making sure each child is the expert on his or her own needs. Goals should be mutually constructed, peer support should be available, and the sociopolitical context of trauma should be emphasized (Elliott et al., 2005). By noting that the child is not at fault for experiencing trauma and that there are larger social forces such as racism and oppression, school social workers can place the experiences of children in a larger context. One example is the detention of immigrant families and separation of children from their parents. By showing support for immigrants and for keeping families together, schools can send the message to children affected by this political issue that they are in a safe place. Peer support could take the form of a buddy program, mentoring arrangements, and social connections for isolated families. Schools are already wonderful places for children to take charge of their exploration, creation, and learning. Creating a trauma-informed school would mean that all children feel able to harness their own power and overcome obstacles caused by traumatic experiences.

Principle 4: Trauma-Informed Services Strive to Maximize a Person's Choice and Control Over Recovery

This principle speaks to the importance of the individual having choice and control over the process of addressing trauma (Elliott et al., 2005). For a child, the prospect of talking about traumatic experiences can be overwhelming. The choice of whom to tell, how much to tell, and when to talk about trauma should be squarely within the child's control. Maximizing choice and control can also take other forms, such as whether the children sit or stand at their desk, what color paper they choose for their artwork, and whether they want to do their math or science homework first. As stated earlier, traumatic events are ones in which we feel powerless and out of control, so re-establishing control, even in small ways, can be very meaningful. In these situations, the school social worker can help all those working with these children find opportunities to maximize their power and feel in control. This could take the form of mediating a discussion between the children and teacher, helping the children voice to parents what they need at home, and working with the administration to find ways for children to have a say in what's happening in the school.

Principle 5: Trauma-Informed Services Are Based in a Relational Collaboration

Building on the principles of empowerment and choice, the fifth principle addresses the importance of relationships. For children who have experienced trauma, relationships can be very scary. People who were supposed to be trustworthy abused their power to violate the child's trust. School social workers must be acutely aware of power dynamics and strive toward collaboration with each child. The helping relationship should be a RICH relationship, providing Respect, Information, Connection, and Hope (Elliott et al., 2005). Children feel respected when they are able to voice their experiences. Providing information about the way trauma affects the brain can challenge their belief that they are "a bad kid." Connection is experienced in a different way between the social worker and the child. The professional and therapeutic relationship focuses on the child's needs alone, and this becomes a corrective experience because other adults have needs and expectations of the child. Finally, the hope that healing is possible and people can be trustworthy is conveyed. In these ways, the RICH relationship becomes the standard for all the interactions in schools. Whether it is the security guard, lunch lady, principal, or classroom teacher, each person the child encounters in a trauma-informed school strives to have a RICH relationship with them.

Principle 6: Trauma-Informed Services Create an Atmosphere That Is Respectful of Survivors' Need for Safety, Respect, and Acceptance

The sixth principle focuses on safety and acceptance. Where the RICH relationship in principle 5 explores one-on-one relationships, this principle takes a broader look at the entire environment. When applying this principle, schools would strive to create a welcoming environment that is also safe and secure. With school shootings and violence in communities creating a need for metal detectors and secure buildings, children must also feel safe as they move about the building and interact with staff and other students. School social workers can assist with this by conducting a safety audit of the physical building to see if there are areas of the school where security is insufficient. Do all the bathroom doors have locks? Are there hallways that are obscured from staff view? Are there crossing guards at busy intersections? Are there lights outside the school at night? Helping with initiatives such as *Safe Routes to Schools* (National Center for Safe Routes to Schools, 2018) and addressing the security concerns in the physical environment would increase the sense of safety in the school for all who enter.

Principle 7: Trauma-Informed Services Emphasize Strengths, Highlighting Adaptations over Symptoms and Resilience Over Pathology

This principle is at the heart of what it means to be trauma-informed. Earlier in this chapter, we asked children the trauma-informed question, "what happened to you?" In following this principle, the school social worker places trauma symptoms in the context of survival and adaptation. Behavior as survival reduces shame and guilt for children, as well as adults. Children who are neglected or abused at home have to be creative and resourceful to get what they need and survive. However, what works at home or in their neighborhoods is typically not as effective in school. Seeing resilience and strengths in children who have endured trauma helps them develop more adaptive ways of engaging with school. It is often the validation of the child's adaptation as a positive behavior that will enable the school social worker to engage an otherwise resistant child in a working alliance toward healing and growth.

Principle 8: The Goal of Trauma-Informed Services Is to Minimize the Possibility of Retraumatization

Since the types of traumatic events experienced by children are so varied and the experience is so unique to each child, it is difficult to identify all the things that could trigger students. However, ensuring that children do not experience another traumatic event in school should be a focus of a trauma-informed program. Abuse of power by educators and other professionals is retraumatizing for children who have been powerless in the face of abuse. Sometimes staff actions and behavioral policies can do more harm than good. School social workers can help with this organizational principle by coordinating response plans for natural disasters, providing crisis counseling after a traumatic event in the community, reaching out to families affected by a recent loss, and helping organize students to provide support to peers and engage in school-wide initiatives such as antibullying campaigns.

Principle 9: Trauma-Informed Services Strive to Be Culturally Competent and to Understand Each Person in the Context of Life Experiences and Cultural Background

The Code of Ethics (National Association of Social Workers, 2008) guides practitioners and clearly states that social workers must strive to understand the influence of culture. This principle of trauma-informed services connects trauma and culture. The meaning one makes of traumatic experiences varies by culture and intersections of identities. School social workers can extend what they already do with students and families in examining the role their culture plays in all aspects of their lives to exploring trauma through this lens as well. School social workers can explore the experience of trauma in the culture of the children they serve and gain a deeper understanding of the unique lived experience of each child and family. It is also important to explore experiences of historical trauma and intergenerational transmission of trauma in families affected by slavery, colonization, genocide, and war. A child who is not a primary survivor of trauma may have similar coping behaviors

---

that are handed down from one generation to the next by grandparents and parents.

Principle 10: Trauma-Informed Agencies Solicit Consumer Input and Involve Consumers in Designing and Evaluating Services

This last principle places value on the voices of service recipients. By sharing their experiences, trauma survivors help to improve on programs for others through the participation in the design and evaluation of services. The creation of "consumer specialist" positions and advisory boards is strongly recommended (Elliott et al., 2005). In the school setting, this means including children in the evaluation of the school. A kids' advisory board could be involved in many of the decisions related to the school environment, activities, and schedules. Many schools have active parent boards or Parent Teacher Associations, but how many actually solicit the feedback of their main "consumer" when making crucial decisions that affect their daily well-being?

The Missing 11th Principle: Addressing Vicarious Trauma

To be truly trauma-informed, organizations must attend to the health and well-being of their workers. Schools are no different. Working in schools means working with children who have been abused, neglected, abandoned, and trafficked. It means becoming acutely aware of children who live in poverty, are homeless and hungry, and are bullied and targeted because of their race, religion, or disability. Working with human beings who have experienced inhumane conditions means that social workers and educators will have normal human reactions to what they come to know and see. Research shows that there are expected and normal reactions to working with children and families who have had stressful or traumatic experiences (Bride, 2007). These reactions are commonly referred to as vicarious trauma, or the taking in of the traumatic experiences of others through empathic professional engagement that has a transformative effect on the worker (Dombo & Gray, 2013). The bio-psycho-social-spiritual impact of the work has real intrapersonal, as well as interpersonal, consequences if left unaddressed. These can take the form of emotional, social, cognitive, and relational changes, as well as decreases in morale and connection to the work that comes from preoccupation with the trauma narratives (Lipsky & Burk, 2009). Providing support and resources to workers in trauma-informed settings can help them be more resilient in the face of trauma.

Conclusion

Implementing the principles of trauma-informed services in school settings may not be as difficult as first imagined. However, this does not mean that there will not be real barriers to implementation. Training and education about trauma take time and financial commitment. Making the link between trauma and poor educational outcomes can help convince administrators that the investment in creating a trauma-informed school will bear fruit not only within the children and families affected by trauma but also within the entire school as behavioral disruptions decrease and attendance rates increase. Trauma-informed schools benefit all children, regardless of survivor status. A school environment where children feel safe, engage in RICH relationships with adults, and have more control over their environment is a positive environment for all children.

Resources

The Joyful Heart Foundation. *Signs of vicarious trauma*. Retrieved from http://www.joyfulheartfoundation.org/learn/vicarious-trauma/identifying-vicarious-trauma/signs-vicarious-trauma
Gives professionals information about the signs and symptoms of vicarious trauma.
National Sexual Violence Resource Center. *Resources for vicarious trauma*. Retrieved from http://www.nsvrc.org/sites/default/files/nsvrc-publications_sane-mobile-app_resources-vicarious-trauma.pdf
Provides information about and numerous resources for addressing vicarious trauma.
Office for Victims of Crime. *The vicarious trauma toolkit*. Retrieved from https://vtt.ovc.ojp.gov
Provides resources and supports for professionals who work with trauma survivors.
Professional Quality of Life. Retrieved from http://www.proqol.org
Provides information about vicarious trauma and strategies for professionals dealing with vicarious trauma. Also provides a self-assessment in the areas of secondary traumatic stress, vicarious resilience, and burnout.

References

Bride, B. E. (2007). Prevalence of secondary traumatic stress among social workers. *Social Work, 52*(1), 63–70.

Dombo, E. A., & Blome, W. W. (2016). Vicarious trauma in child welfare workers: An organizational study. *Journal of Public Child Welfare, 10*(5), 505–523.

Dombo, E. A., & Gray, C. (2013). Engaging spirituality in addressing vicarious trauma in clinical social work: A self-care model. *Social Work and Christianity, 40*(1), 89–104.

Elliot, D., Bjelajac, P., Fallot, R., Markoff, L., & Reed, B. (2005). Trauma-informed or trauma-denied: Principles and implementation of trauma-informed services for women. *Journal of Community Psychology, 33*(4), 461–477.

Holmes, C., Levy, M., Smith, A., Pinne, S., & Neese, P. (2015). A model for creating a supportive trauma-informed culture for children in preschool settings. *Journal of Child and Family Studies, 24,* 1650–1659.

Lipsky, L., & Burk. C. (2009). *Trauma stewardship: An everyday guide to caring for self while caring for others.* San Francisco, CA: Berrett-Koehler Publishers.

National Association of Social Workers (NASW). (2008). *The code of ethics of the National Association of Social Workers.* Washington, DC: NASW Press.

National Center for Safe Routes to Schools. (2018). *Safe routes.* Retrieved from http://www.saferoutesinfo.org

Saunders, B. E., & Adams, Z. W. (2014). Epidemiology of traumatic experiences in childhood. *Child and Adolescent Psychiatric Clinics of North America, 23*(2), 167–184.

6

Evidence-Supported, Trauma-Focused Interventions

Providing trauma-informed interventions in a school-based setting is helpful because parents are often unable to get their children to service providers in the community because of barriers such as cost, distance, and time away from work and caring for other family members (Shamblin, Graham, & Bianco, 2016). School social workers can help children heal from trauma through the provision of a number of trauma-sensitive interventions. This chapter offers an overview of some current, empirically supported interventions for use in direct practice with children and adolescents in school settings.

The chapter is divided by developmental stages to provide appropriate strategies for preschool, elementary, middle, and high school students. The interventions are the Attachment, Self-Regulation, and Competency (ARC) framework (Blaustein & Kinniburgh, 2010); Trauma-Focused Cognitive Behavioral Therapy (TF-CBT) for children (Mannarino et al., 2012); Cognitive Behavioral Intervention for Trauma in Schools (CBITS) group intervention (Stein et al., 2003); and Structured Psychotherapy for Adolescents Responding to Chronic Stress (SPARCS) group intervention for older adolescents (Habib, Labruna, & Neuman, 2013). Case examples will be provided to demonstrate how these interventions are used in practice.

Attachment, Self-Regulation, and Competency Framework

Margaret Blaustein and Kristine Kinniburgh developed the ARC framework to assist children and adolescents who have experienced trauma. Based on concepts from attachment, developmental, and trauma theories, the ARC framework targets the complex neurological, psychological, behavioral, and social impacts of complex, developmental, and relational trauma (Blaustein

& Kinniburgh, 2010). When the ARC framework was first developed, the diagnostic formulation of posttraumatic stress disorder (PTSD) in the DSM-IV-TR was limited to experiences that involved physical injury or threat to physical integrity, witnessing death or the threat of one's own death (American Psychiatric Association, 2000). This narrow definition of traumatic events left out experiences that are traumatizing to children such as separation from attachment figures, neglect, emotional abuse, and having caregivers who were distracted and not attentive because of their own psychosocial impairments (Blaustein & Kinniburgh, 2010). The concept of *complex trauma* was created to explain these kinds of experiences (Courtois, 2004), as was the effort to create a new diagnosis of developmental trauma (van der Kolk, 2005). Left unaddressed by the concept of PTSD were difficulties with affect regulation, attention and consciousness, difficulty relating to others, somatization, guilt and shame, and chronic hopelessness and despair (Courtois, 2004). These presentations did not fit with the fear, helplessness, and horror that were part of the PTSD formulation in the DSM-IV-TR (American Psychiatric Association, 2000). The DSM-5 has a developmental subtype for children six years old and younger (American Psychiatric Association, 2013), but school social workers must be mindful that many of the issues related to complex trauma are not accounted for in this formulation.

The ARC framework was developed to address developmental and complex trauma through a model of core components with targeted areas for intervention designed to be flexible enough for implementation across practice settings (Arvidson et al., 2011; Blaustein & Kinniburgh, 2010). There are three core domains and ten building blocks:

Attachment—all caregivers in the child's life are included in this
   domain. In order to create safer and more attuned relationships with
   the attachment figures in the child's life, caregivers need to change
   their behavior as well. The areas of focus ("building blocks") for the
   caregivers are:
   Caregiver management of affect—education is provided to caregivers to
      help them improve their skills in managing their own behavior as well
      as their reactions to the child's behavior.
   Attunement—teaches the caregiver how to recognize what the child
      needs emotionally when their behavior is distressing and how to
      respond to soothe and calm them.

Consistent response—tools are provided to the caregiver so that they can provide the child with consistent, appropriate, and attuned responses.

Routines and rituals—because safety is increased with routines and predictability, caregivers are supported in developing schedules and routines.

Self-Regulation—this domain focuses on the child's responses to stress and overwhelming emotions. Children are taught how to identify what they are feeling, how to regulate how they respond to feelings, and ways to communicate responses safely and effectively. There are three building blocks:

Affect identification—helping students learn how to recognize their distressed physical and emotional cues and put words to their somatic and emotive actions.

Modulation—creating strategies with children to help them tolerate and manage different feeling states.

Affect expression—learning new words and language to express strong emotions so that students can safely share their feelings and connect with others.

Competency—the third domain explores achieving the necessary developmental skills to be on par with their peers academically and socially. As many children who experience complex trauma focus on survival, they often do not develop confidence in themselves. The two building blocks in this domain are:

Executive functions—the capacity to plan, organize, and execute tasks is often difficult for children who have experienced trauma, so this building block focuses on the skills and tasks needed for the child to connect the behavior with the desired outcome.

Self-development—the child is assisted with the development of a positive sense of self and a future-oriented outlook on life. There is also a focus on producing a life story, or narrative, to explore the past.

Trauma Experience Integration—the last building block combines all the others into specific, developmentally appropriate, strategies for healing from trauma.

Applying the ARC framework with children and families in schools is flexible and adaptable, is culturally adaptable, and is effective with young children (Arvidson et al., 2011).

Cognitive Behavioral Intervention for Trauma in Schools

As a group intervention geared to support children who have been exposed to traumatic events, CBITS has been in use in US schools since 2000 and was adapted for international use (Little, Akin-Little, & Somerville, 2011). CBITS focuses on alleviating PTSD symptomatology, depression, and anxiety through skill-building in the areas of relaxation, challenging upsetting thoughts, social problem-solving, and learning how to process traumatic memories and grief (Jaycox, 2004; Jaycox et al., 2012). CBITS is typically used for children between grades six and nine (ages 10 to 15) and incorporates a holistic framework by including separate parent and teacher education sessions as part of the program. The six distinct cognitive behavioral techniques that are taught to children are:

- Education about PTSD and normal reactions to trauma
- Relaxation training with breathing exercises to help manage anxiety
- Therapy that focuses on cognitive distortions and developing adaptive thoughts
- Gradual, real-life exposure to the experiences or people that cause fear in order to develop mastery over the fears
- Stress or trauma exposure that uses imagery to gradually approach traumatic memories and manage feelings that arise
- Social problem-solving to help with anger and impulsivity, as well as managing interactions with others

Child participants of CBITS attend ten group sessions with peers (averaging seven children per group) and individualized sessions (timed before exposure exercises) to achieve these skills. Group sessions are usually conducted for an hour once a week within a school setting, though CBITS has been delivered in mental health clinic settings as well. Screening for the intervention is done through the utilization of several assessments: the Life Events Scale (to determine the child's level of exposure to violence); the Child PTSD Symptom Scale as well as the Children's Depression Inventory (completed by the child to determine scored clinical levels of PTSD and depression); and the Pediatric Symptom Checklist (completed by the child's parent or guardian to determine the child's level of functioning before treatment). Research shows that CBITS is effective in helping children decrease depressive symptoms and improve problematic behavior (Cohen & Mannarino, 2010).

Trauma-Focused Cognitive Behavioral Therapy

TF-CBT is a modules-based model of psychotherapy originally developed for children with PTSD symptoms, depression, behavior problems, and other difficulties related to traumatic life experiences (Cohen, Mannarino, & Deblinger, 2006). This treatment is a short-term approach to alleviating a child's presentations of maladapted behaviors and can be implemented in as few as 12 sessions, though longer periods of time work as well. TF-CBT has been empirically shown to result in improvements in depression, anxiety, behavioral problems, trauma-related shame, interpersonal trust, and social competence and is one of few evidence-based practices in trauma treatment (Little, Akin-Little, & Somerville, 2011). TF-CBT's working modules can be summarized using the acronym *PRACTICE*:

- **P**sychoeducation is provided about the impact of trauma and common reactions
- **R**elaxation and stress management skills are individualized for each child
- **A**ffective expression and modulation are taught for emotional coping and regulation
- **C**ognitive coping and processing are utilized to address thoughts, feelings, and behaviors to modify inaccurate beliefs about the trauma
- **T**rauma narration is used in which the child describes his or her personal traumatic experiences
- **I**n vivo mastery of trauma reminders is used to help overcome avoidance
- **C**onjoint sessions with family and significant people are provided
- **E**nhancing future safety and enriching skills are used to generalize to other environments

For treatment to be effective, the school social worker implementing TF-CBT must be mindful of and operate concurrently with a family's religious, cultural, and community values because the intervention is with both the child and the parents or guardians (Scheeringa et al., 2011). The practitioner provides the following three treatment "phases" to complete therapy: (1) desensitizing and skills-building stage to improve a child's affective, behavioral, biological, and cognitive self-regulation, and parenting interventions to enhance caregiver coping, behavioral management skills, and support of

---

the child; (2) trauma narrative phase during which children describe and cognitively process their personal trauma experiences; and (3) treatment closure steps, including conjoint caregiver-child sessions and safety planning (Mannarino et al., 2012). During each of these phases of TF-CBT, the social worker must model trust, empathy, and acceptance for the child so that the child may begin to restore trust and internal functioning (Little, Akin-Little, & Somerville, 2011). Research on the effectiveness of TF-CBT has shown that it helps improve dysregulated behavior, lower rates of dissociation and depression, and improve parenting skills (Cohen & Mannarino, 2010). Box 6.1 depicts the use of TF-CBT in David's Story, and Skill Box 6.1 provides more detail on the Flipping Your Lid intervention.

Box 6.1 David's Story

Trauma Type: Episodes of homelessness, incarcerated attachment figure, death of an attachment figure
Culture/Ethnicity: African American

Presenting Problem
David is a ten-year-old, African American boy who is currently in fifth grade at a local elementary school. He lives with his mother, grandmother, and aunt. David's father was incarcerated for much of his life and was recently released from jail. However, David's father died unexpectedly shortly after being released. Since his father's abrupt death, David has presented with volatile mood and intermittent angry outbursts at school and at home. David demonstrates multiple signs of arousal, including difficulty sleeping, impaired concentration, intrusive thoughts, and irritability. David is diagnosed with attention deficit hyperactivity disorder (ADHD), for which he takes medication. David reported suicidal ideation when he was nine years old due to bullying at school but denies a plan or intent. David is connected with the mental health team at his school for services.

Background/History
David is an only child and has been raised by his mother, primarily, with support from his grandmother and aunt. David's father was

---

incarcerated for most of his life, but they developed a strong relationship through visitation and phone calls. Throughout David's childhood he and his mother experienced several episodes of homelessness and stayed in local family shelters for several weeks at a time. This is David's first year at this elementary school, and he has been in three different schools in the past three years. David has also witnessed significant community violence, as evidenced by his report of having witnessed gun violence and knowing someone who had been stabbed.

Reason for Referral

Since his father's death, David has been struggling in school, as evidenced by angry outbursts with classmates and staff, use of humor to distract classmates, and difficulty with concentration. David is currently receiving services from his elementary school's mental health team but was referred to the Trauma-Focused Cognitive Behavioral Therapy (TF-CBT) groups offered by an outside agency for additional support. David attends the weekly TF-CBT groups and has practiced feeling identification, which has helped him build his affect regulation skills. David is also able to utilize and explain the hand model of the brain and how it relates to stress and the body. With a stronger sense of his triggers, feelings, and ways to help calm himself, David has been able to collaborate with the counselors to create a trauma narrative detailing the loss of his father. Through participation in the TF-CBT group, David has had fewer behavioral issues at school and at home and has been able to better manage his symptoms of arousal, such as difficulty sleeping, impaired concentration, and intrusive thoughts.

Skill Box 6.1 "Flipping Your Lid"

Dr. Dan Siegel coined the term "flipping your lid" to describe what happens in our brains when we become stressed, are presented with a threat, or are reminded of stressors from the past (https://www.youtube.com/watch?v=f-m2YcdMdFw). When a person "flips their lid" it means that they are no longer thinking or acting clearly. To help explain this to children, you can use the hand to create a model of the brain. The palm and wrist of the hand represent the reptilian brain. The reptilian brain controls the body's automatic functions, such as breathing or our heart rate. If you cross the thumb over your palm, this represents the limbic system, specifically the amygdala, which serves as the body's alarm system. When faced with a threat, the amygdala comes online, and we respond with our fight, flight, freeze, or faint responses. Threats can include immediate stressors in our environment or past stressful memories. The four remaining fingers cover the thumb and represent the cortex or our "thinking brain." The cortex is the thinking, problem-solving part of our brain. When the cortex is covering the limbic system, we are able to think logically and exercise self-control. When we are presented with a threat, the cortex goes offline, resulting in us "flipping our lid" and responding with our automatic limbic system responses. When working with children, we can use the hand model of the brain to teach children about how stress affects our functioning. The goals of the interventions outlined in this chapter are to help kids to learn how to identify triggers and threats in their environment and to develop skills to help bring the "thinking brain" back online using affect regulation and relaxation techniques.

Structured Psychotherapy for Adolescents Responding to Chronic Stress

Delivered in a group format lasting 22 sessions, the SPARCS intervention is designed to help adolescents ages 12 to 18 develop a strengths-based response to chronic trauma. It utilizes techniques from Dialectical Behavioral Therapy to help with the *Four C's*: cultivating awareness, coping effectively, connecting with others, and creating meaning and purpose (Habib, LaBruna, & Newman, 2013). The intervention targets six domains:

- Emotional regulation and impulsivity
- Self-perception
- Physical health and somatization
- Relationships

- Attention/consciousness
- Developing a sense of purpose and meaning in life

These domains are addressed in the group sessions through role plays, discussion, excerpts from movies and television shows, mindfulness, and other activities (Habib, LaBruna, & Newman, 2013). Studies on effectiveness have shown that SPARCS helps adolescents improve relationships with others, lower incidents of behavioral problems, and reduce symptoms of anxiety and depression (Cohen & Mannarino, 2010). However, many adolescents do not seek services in their school because of perceived stigma around accessing mental health services (van de Water et al., 2018). Consequently, school social workers need to be creative in ways to interest students and implement SPARCS groups, including conducting them off campus in the community.

With multiple evidence-based, culturally responsive, and age-appropriate interventions to choose from, school social workers have many options for integrating trauma-responsive interventions in their schools.

Resources

Attachment, Regulation, and Competency (ARC). Retrieved from https://arcframework.org
This website is managed by the creators of the ARC, Margaret Blaustein and Kristine Kinniburgh. It has resources for service providers, families, and communities regarding the use of the ARC framework. It also provides information about trauma and resilience. There are specific links on the website for kids and teens to help demystify treatment that uses the ARC framework.
Treatment Services and Adaptation Center: Resiliency, Hope and Wellness in Schools Cognitive Behavioral Intervention for Trauma in Schools (CBITS). Retrieved from https://traumaawareschools.org/cbits
This website provides resources, fact sheets, and training for professionals to learn how to deliver the CBITS intervention. It also offers videos and guidelines for teachers, parents, and youths on a wide variety of trauma-related topics.
National Child Traumatic Stress Network TF-CBT WEB. Retrieved from https://www.nctsn.org/resources/tf-cbt-web
NCTSN and its partners developed this free resource to provide online training for mental health professionals to learn how to use TF-CBT.
Trauma-Focused Cognitive Behavioral Therapy (TF-CBT). Retrieved from https://tfcbt.org
This website is offered from the founders of TF-CBT, Drs. Cohen, Deblinger, and Mannarino. It provides implementation resources, training, and certification.
Structured Psychotherapy for Adolescents Responding to Chronic Stress (SPARCS). Retrieved from http://sparcstraining.com/index.php

The founders of the SPARCS group intervention, Drs. Habib and Labruna, provide this website for mental health professionals to access information about the intervention and opportunities for training.

References

American Psychiatric Association. (2000). *Diagnostic and statistical manual of mental disorders* (4th ed., text rev.). Washington, DC: Author.

American Psychiatric Association. (2013). *Diagnostic and statistical manual of mental disorders* (5th ed.). Arlington, VA: American Psychiatric Publishing.

Arvidson, J., Kinniburgh, K., Howard, K., Spinazzola, J., Strothers, H., Evans, M., Andres, B., Cohen, C., & Blaustein, M. E. (2011). Treatment of complex trauma in young children: Developmental and cultural considerations in application of the ARC Intervention Model. *Journal of Child & Adolescent Trauma, 4*(1), 34–51.

Blaustein, M. E., & Kinniburgh, K. M. (2010). *Treating traumatic stress in children and adolescents: How to foster resilience through attachment, self-regulation, and competency.* New York, NY: The Guilford Press.

Cohen, J. A., Mannarino, A. P., & Deblinger, E. (2006). *Treating trauma and traumatic grief in children and adolescents.* New York, NY: The Guilford Press.

Cohen, J. A., & Mannarino, A. P. (2010). Psychotherapeutic options for traumatized children. *Current Opinion in Pediatrics, 22*(5), 605–609.

Courtois, C. A. (2004). Complex trauma, complex reactions: Assessment and treatment. *Psychotherapy: Theory, Research, Practice, Training, 41*(4), 412–425.

Habib, M., Labruna, V., & Newman, J. (2013). Complex histories and complex presentations: Implementation of a manually-guided group treatment for traumatized adolescents. *Journal of Family Violence, 28*, 717–728.

Jaycox, L. H. (2004). *Cognitive behavioral intervention for trauma in schools.* Longmont, CO: Sopris West.

Jaycox, L. H., Kataoka, S. H., Stein, B. D., Langley, A. K., & Wong, M. (2012). Cognitive behavioral intervention for trauma in schools. *Journal of Applied School Psychology, 28*(3), 239–255.

Little, S. G., Akin-Little, A., & Somerville, M. P. (2011). Response to trauma in children: An examination of effective intervention and post-traumatic growth. *School Psychology International, 32*(5), 448–463.

Mannarino, A. P., Cohen, J. A., Deblinger, E., Runyon, M. K., & Steer, R. A. (2012). Trauma-Focused Cognitive-Behavioral Therapy for children: Sustained impact of treatment 6 and 12 months later. *Child Maltreatment, 17*(3), 231–241.

Scheeringa, M. S., Weems, C. F., Cohen, J. A., Amaya-Jackson, L., & Guthrie, D. (2011). Trauma-Focused Cognitive Behavioral Therapy for posttraumatic stress disorder in three- through six-year-old children: A randomized clinical trial. *Journal of Child Psychology and Psychiatry, 52*(8), 853–860.

Shamblin, S., Graham, D., & Bianco, J. A. (2016). Creating trauma-informed schools for rural Appalachia: The Partnerships Program for enhancing resiliency, confidence, and workforce development in early childhood education. *School Mental Health, 8,* 189–200.

Stein, B. D., Jaycox, L. H., Kataoka, S. H., Wong, M., Tu, W., Eliot, M. N., & Fink, A. (2003). A mental health intervention for school children exposed to violence: A randomized controlled trial. *Journal of the American Medical Association, 290*(5), 603–611.

van de Water, T. V., Rossouw, J., van der Watt, A. S., Yadin, E., & Seedat, S. (2018). Adolescents' experience of stigma when accessing school-based PTSD interventions. *Qualitative Health Research, 28*(7), 1088–1098.

van der Kolk, B. (2005). Developmental trauma disorder: Toward a rational diagnosis for children with complex trauma histories. *Psychiatric Annals, 35*(5), 401–408.

7

■■■

Engaging Teachers, Families, and Kids in Creating Trauma-Informed School Environments

This chapter explores the essential framework for creating a customized model for schools that engages all stakeholders in this paradigm shift. Models of trauma-informed schools will be reviewed, as well as lessons learned from other areas of social work practice, such as child welfare and mental health (Ko et al., 2008). Case examples will demonstrate how to implement the strategies and how the strategies can affect children.

Where to Begin? Shifting Schools to Trauma-Informed Environments

Based on the research presented in previous chapters, it would stand to reason that transforming schools into trauma-informed settings will help children, teachers, and schools achieve targeted educational outcomes (Perry & Daniels, 2016). School social workers are uniquely suited to shepherd this process because it requires coordination and collaboration with multiple systems (Walkley & Cox, 2013) while remaining focused on the social, emotional, behavioral, and academic needs of the children. This will not happen overnight, or even in one academic year, so long-term planning with several phases will support sustainable change (Phifer & Hull, 2016).

To begin laying groundwork for this effort, each school must think through the stakeholders who need to commit to and support the initiative. These may include the school superintendent, local lawmakers, the principal, teachers' union leaders, parent association leaders, student government, and others. Another key factor is identifying collaborators in the community who are in the position to provide necessary resources (Holmes et al., 2015). Schools cannot be all things to all children, and partnering with organizations in the community that specialize in trauma, mental health, behavioral health, and family services enriches the programs and extends the reach of these efforts (Shamblin, Graham, & Bianco, 2016). After the stakeholders and collaborators have been identified, they must work together to articulate clear messages around their shared vision for a trauma-informed school (Chafouleas et al., 2016). For most schools, developing a multitiered framework on which services are built will be most helpful (Dorado et al., 2016; Perry & Daniels, 2016; Shamblin, Graham, & Bianco, 2016).

In some cases, there will be resistance to this initiative, as there has been in the past with regard to changing the culture in schools (Walkley & Cox, 2013). Schools must grapple with the tension between their primary focus on education and the way trauma interferes with it (Ko et al., 2008). Helping schools to understand, anticipate, and respond to children who have experienced trauma with curiosity rather than discipline is a major shift (Cummings, Addante, Swindell, & Meadan, 2017). However, helping constituents understand the impact of trauma on learning and, more important, helping stakeholders understand the importance of safe school environments for *all* children is possible through education and training. In schools, one of the largest groups of stakeholders are the teachers. Their support for, or resistance to, an initiative makes all the difference. Securing their support early and soliciting their participation and input in the process are key. This can be achieved through:

- Establishing the link between untreated trauma and academic difficulties
- Limiting the time students spend outside the classroom for services
- Improving communication between teachers and support service personnel
- Providing more training and education about trauma to teachers

Some schools develop participation by using Professional Learning Communities. Grade-level teacher groups discuss specific content area concerns and are then encouraged to apply a trauma lens by asking what else is known about a student or what else might be going on with a child that interferes with academic progress. The teachers may not know, but asking the questions is an important step in the right direction. By attending to teacher approval and support, school social workers create a trauma-informed school in these ways and increase chances of long-term success (Baweja et al., 2016).

Basic Assumptions of Trauma-Informed Approaches

In providing guidance on how to create trauma-informed systems of care, the Substance Abuse and Mental Health Services Administration (SAMHSA) outlines four key assumptions that everyone in the system must adopt for true integration (SAMHSA, 2014). These assumptions are a good place to start when establishing the message and vision for a trauma-informed school. These are considered the *Four R's*:

- *Realize*—all stakeholders must realize that trauma has a significant impact on the children in their school and demonstrate an understanding that the behavioral and educational problems can be addressed by addressing the trauma.
- *Recognize*—efforts to recognize the signs of trauma can be achieved through screening and assessing all children in the school. Training for all adults who work with students will also help them recognize the signs of trauma.
- *Respond*—the school's response to the impact of trauma on learning is to create a trauma-informed school that implements all its principles and designs a framework to meet its own unique needs.
- *Resist retraumatization*—this key assumption connects to the awareness that trauma may be triggered by certain practices and settings, even inadvertently, by well-meaning teachers and administrators. In creating a trauma-informed school, the goal is to minimize the chances of children's current or past trauma being triggered by something that happens in school.

Individual schools must think through these four R's and the assumptions they are making in their setting. These will guide the rest of the implementation process (Overstreet & Chafouleas, 2016).

Implementation of Trauma-Informed Approaches

Much of the literature on creating trauma-informed schools recommends the use of a multitiered approach for service delivery because this is a familiar model in schools (Phifer & Hull, 2016). There are three tiers. The primary tier universally addresses system-wide issues around safety and prevention. The secondary tier is focused on small groups of identified students who require moderate interventions. The tertiary tier targets specific students who need individualized and intensive support. Sugai and Horner (2009) outline six distinguishing features of a three-tier framework previously used in school settings:

1. Evidence-supported practices are employed.
2. The intensity of support increases with each tier.
3. Decisions about which students receive supports are rooted in data-based and problem-solving frameworks.
4. The response of students to the supports they receive influences modifications.
5. Fidelity to treatment protocols is measured for optimal maintenance.
6. Early detection and referral to services are achieved.

Each tier applies the six features moving from universally applied interventions with low-intensity in tier 1, to more targeted, moderately intensive interventions in tier 2, and finally to highly intense interventions targeted to selected students who require ongoing support (Chafouleas et al., 2016). Chapter 6 explored some examples of evidence-supported interventions that can be considered for use in this multitiered framework.

Example 1: Preschool Setting

The scholarly literature on trauma-informed schools provides some examples of implementation that are of particular usefulness when contemplating what will work for each individual school. Beginning with preschool settings, Holmes et al. (2015) explore the creation of a Head Start Trauma Smart (HSTS) partnership between a mental health center and three Head Start programs in a Midwestern state serving children three to five years old in one city-center community. Their goal was for HSTS to be an organization-wide effort and reduce the chances of retraumatization. They utilized the Attachment, Self-Regulation, and Competency (ARC) model, Trauma-Focused Cognitive Behavioral Therapy (TF-CBT), and mental health consultation specifically designed for early childhood. The main components developed to structure HSTS were:

Tier 1: Training for everyone who will encounter a child in the program, in the community, and in the child's home. This is so that everyone has the same information and knowledge and can be addressing the children in the same manner.

Tier 2: Classroom consultations conducted for specific children to support the teacher in the class environment. During these visits, the HSTS therapist is able to help the teacher with skills and help set up a classroom space that is trauma-informed. This may include finding space in the room for a dysregulated child to use calming techniques. Peer-based mentoring is also part of this Tier of services, in which parents and teachers are able to mentor each other and continue to learn best practices in applying skills and knowledge.

Tier 3: Children who are referred for services receive intensive therapy that utilizes a trauma-informed, evidence-supported intervention. Referrals can come from teachers, parents, or staff. Given the age and developmental stage of the children, sessions are shorter, but more sessions are provided. For example, a session may last only 30 minutes and the child has 24 sessions. Parent participation in therapy is highly encouraged, and communication between parents and therapists is facilitated through home visits, phone calls, and notes home after sessions. Parents are also given strategies to use outside sessions to bolster what is being done in the therapy.

Research conducted on the outcomes in the HSTS program found that the children who received tier 3 services showed improvements in attention, decreases in oppositional and externalizing behaviors, and fewer issues with hyperactivity. They also found that classroom environments scored more positively on measures of climate and relationship quality (Holmes et al., 2015).

For school social workers serving rural school districts, Shamblin et al. (2016) discuss how to create trauma-informed schools through community partnerships. They describe ways to leverage shared resources to support the needs of teachers and children. Their research on a three-tiered community partnership consultation model found improvement in teacher confidence to affect challenging child behaviors, a decrease in negative elements in the learning environment, and increased teacher ratings of child resilience. Their model provides workforce development in rural areas and at the same time enhances child resilience as seen in measures of self-control, attachment, and initiative in the study. In both the urban and rural areas, providing direct services as well as indirect consultation services in the school afforded an otherwise inaccessible service to families and schools in need.

Example 2: Elementary School Setting

Perry and Daniels (2016) report on the implementation of three trauma-informed strategies in one pre-K–8, Title 1 school within the City of New Haven, Connecticut. They created the New Haven Trauma Coalition (NHTC), which comprised community mental health agencies, local politicians, and public school administrators. The interventions chosen were the Cognitive Behavioral Intervention for Trauma in the Schools (CBITS) for groups of children and Care Coordination for specific children and their families. The main components of the pilot program were:

Tier 1: Professional development was provided to all personnel in the school to increase their understanding of trauma and the impact on learning, teach trauma-informed practices and services, and effect behavior change in the classrooms. A main focus of the two-day training was on helping teachers create strategies for utilizing trauma-informed approaches in their everyday interactions with students, such as de-escalation techniques. Self-care strategies and small group discussions about the new initiative were also part of the training.

Tier 2: Classroom workshops were held to discuss the initiative with select groups of students, encouraging discussion about the ways in which stress affects learning. These students were empowered to participate in selecting the topics they wanted to learn about, and therefore the three-day workshops were tailored to their interests and needs. There were also activities related to trust, coping, peer relationships, mindfulness, and stress responses.

Tier 3: Specific families were identified for the Care Coordination services based on their need. These families received communication regarding the trauma-informed services and improved the relationship between the school and the families through coordination of care for services that met the complex needs of the family. In addition, students who required more intensive therapeutic interventions in school were identified and chosen to participate in the CBITS ten-week group treatment. These students were able to learn new ways to cope and received psychoeducation about trauma. Their family members were also given handouts each week that their child was receiving the intervention.

This pilot program is a great example of the beginning stages of implementation and ways to start off small with this big idea of transforming a school into a trauma-informed environment. The NHTC demonstrated an ability to increase knowledge about trauma for the school personnel, offer support in identifying children and families in need of more intensive care, provide Care Coordination and the CBITS intervention for select families and students, and shift the pilot school to a trauma-informed system (Perry & Daniels, 2016).

Example 3: Elementary Schools in Communities of Color

A third example of implementation comes from Dorado and colleagues (2016) with regard to the Healthy Environments and Response to Trauma in Schools (HEARTS) program from the University of California, San Francisco (UCSF). The leaders of the San Francisco Unified School District (SFUSD) prioritized addressing the "school to prison pipeline" dynamic in their district because they were seeing students with disabilities and students of color experiencing higher rates of suspension and expulsion and higher rates of engagement with the juvenile justice system and prison. High levels of community violence and widespread experiences of racial bias affected the students in these San Francisco schools, and many students had other traumatic experiences as well. The collaboration between UCSF and SFUSD was created to address many complex and interrelated problems. The main goals were to:

- Increase student engagement in school and student wellness
- Increase staff knowledge of trauma and their ability to create trauma-informed classrooms
- Support teachers and staff through addressing secondary exposure to trauma and preventing burnout
- Rectify the disproportional application of suspensions and expulsions of children of color

The interventions utilized were crisis support and trauma-focused therapy. The main components of the HEARTS program across four different schools were:

Tier 1: All school personnel received training on trauma and trauma-informed services workshops to gain an understanding of how trauma affects learning. They also received training on burnout prevention and self-care. For parents and caregivers of students, psychoeducation about trauma and training on skills for coping with stress were offered universally. All students received in-class training on coping.

Tier 2: The issue of disproportionate application of discipline for students of color was addressed through consultation with school leaders and revision of policies and practices. These efforts led to the creation of alternatives to suspension through Coordinated Care and more trauma-informed behavior plans. Wellness services were offered to teachers to address the impact of trauma exposure. Students at risk were identified and offered psychoeducation and skills training.

Tier 3: Trauma-specific therapy was offered to targeted students with more severe mental health concerns related to trauma. This work was coordinated with the Individualized Education Plan (IEP), and clinicians worked collaboratively with teachers and parents. Parents were encouraged to engage in the treatment and were offered supports, and teachers and staff who were negatively affected by the work were given short-term supports. If more intensive supports were needed, referrals were made. On a system-wide level, the process for addressing mental health needs of students improved.

By addressing the role that culture plays in trauma-informed services, the SFUSD schools were able to highlight disciplinary practices that had disproportionate negative effects on students of color. Layering the understanding of trauma with cultural humility allowed the schools to change disciplinary practices that were retraumatizing for some students and that sent others into juvenile justice and prison systems. The evaluation of the HEARTS implementation shows that school engagement increased, staff understanding of trauma increased, student behavioral problems decreased, and suspension of students outside of school decreased. Finally, for those students receiving intensive psychotherapy for their trauma, there were improvements in affect regulation and decreases in symptoms of trauma (Dorado et al., 2016).

Lessons Learned

Schools are not the only systems striving to become responsive to the needs of trauma survivors, and there are some lessons to be learned from other service arenas. Notably, Ko and colleagues (2008) offered some guidance on making services more trauma-informed. In all sectors, beginning with training and education is recommended. Educators, first responders, child welfare workers, health care providers, and law enforcement officials would

---

benefit from education regarding the signs and symptoms of trauma, training in screening protocols, and knowledge about resources for trauma-informed mental health care. In child welfare systems, this training should extend to foster parents, adoptive parents, and professionals working in the courts. First responders, namely police officers, also require more guidance on how to manage a dysregulated child or adult, families in crisis, and containment strategies when intervening while a traumatic event is occurring. For health care workers, understanding the somatic expression of trauma can help in identifying their patients who may require more supports and services. As more systems become trauma-informed, the environments children encounter outside of school will begin to feel safer. Lucas's Story in Box 7.1 is an illustration of providing services in a school setting that address both academic and familial challenges.

Box 7.1 Lucas's Story

Trauma Type: Witness to domestic violence and substance abuse by attachment figure
Culture/Ethnicity: Latino

Presenting Problem

Lucas is a ten-year-old Latino boy who is currently in fifth grade at a local elementary school. Lucas lives with his mother, father, and younger sister, but his mother and father are separated. Lucas has witnessed his father's substance abuse at home, as well as several serious medical injuries as a result of his use. Lucas reports that he experiences persistent intrusive thoughts about his father and home life, which have been affecting his concentration in school and disrupting his sleep. Lucas is connected with the mental health team at his school for services.

Background/History

Lucas has lived with his mother, father, and younger sister for his whole life. For as long as Lucas can remember, his father has abused alcohol. Lucas, his mother, and his sister share one of the bedrooms of their two-bedroom apartment, while his father uses the other. Lucas recalls several

---

instances when he and his mother came home to find his father on the floor with blood surrounding him as a result of an accident due to his alcohol use. Lucas describes a close relationship with his mother but often worries about his family's well-being. It's important to Lucas's mother that their community does not know about his father's substance use, which has limited Lucas's community supports. Lucas has always been a good student in school, as evidenced by his grades and good reports on behavior. However, Lucas has struggled to pay attention and concentrate in class for the past year, which has affected his school work.

Reason for Referral

Lucas is currently receiving services from his elementary school's mental health team but was referred to the Trauma-Focused Cognitive Behavioral Therapy (TF-CBT) groups offered by an outside agency to help address the impact of his home life and father's substance use on his presentation at school. Lucas attends the weekly TF-CBT group and is actively engaged. He demonstrates understanding of how stress affects the brain and how this relates to thoughts, feelings, and behavior. Lucas has learned various affect regulation and cognitive coping skills that focus on replacing negative thoughts with more positive thoughts. He has been eager to share about his personal experience. With proper support, Lucas collaborated with one of the clinicians to complete a trauma narrative about his father's substance use. Through participation in the TF-CBT group, Lucas has been able to pay attention better in class and manage his intrusive thoughts better with the skills he learned in group.

Resources

Helping Traumatized Children Learn: Supportive School Environments for Children Traumatized by Family Violence (2005).

Helping Traumatized Children Learn: Creating and Advocating for Trauma-Sensitive Schools (2013). Retrieved from https://traumasensitiveschools.org

These reports, from the Massachusetts Advocates for Children, Trauma, and Learning Policy Initiative in collaboration with Harvard Law School's Task Force on Children Affected by Domestic Violence, introduce the Flexible Framework "to help schools weave trauma sensitivity into all the activities of the school day" through "six discrete but interrelated school operations: (1) leadership, (2) professional development, (3) access to resources and services, (4) academic and nonacademic strategies, (5) policies, procedures and protocols, and (6) collaboration with families" (2013, p. 12).

The second volume expands the Flexible Framework by discussing how "becoming trauma sensitive requires not only a deep understanding of trauma's impact on learning but also a spirit of inquiry that most often starts with a small but enthusiastic group of leaders and staff who learn together and can articulate their sense of urgency about why they feel trauma sensitivity will provide better education outcomes for all students" (2015, p. 12).

Both volumes include an extensive set of annotative references for seeking out additional scholarship and research on a wide range of trauma-related topics.

Trauma-Informed Schools Learning Network for Girls of Color. Retrieved from http://schools4girlsofcolor.org

This website provides free information about trauma-informed approaches in schools for girls of color as well as current resources available to members of the Learning Network.

References

Baweja, S., Santiago, C. D., Vona, P., Pears, G., Langley, A., & Kataoka, S. (2016). Improving implementation of a school-based program for traumatized students: Identifying factors that promote teacher support and collaboration. *School Mental Health, 8*, 120–131.

Chafouleas, S. M., Johnson, A. H., Overstreet, S., & Santos, N. M. (2016). Toward a blueprint for trauma-informed service delivery in schools. *School Mental Health, 8*, 144–162.

Cummings, K. P., Addante, S., Swindell, J., & Meadan, H. (2017). Creating supportive environments for children who have had exposure to traumatic events. *Journal of Child and Family Studies, 26*, 2728–2741.

Dorado, J. S., Martinez, M., McArthur, L. E., & Leibovitz, T. (2016). Healthy Environments and Response to Trauma in Schools (HEARTS): A whole-school, multi-level, prevention and intervention program for creating trauma-informed, safe and supportive schools. *School Mental Health, 8*, 163–167.

Holmes, C., Levy, M., Smith, A., Pinne, S., & Neese, P. (2015). A model for creating a supportive trauma-informed culture for children in preschool settings. *Journal of Child and Family Studies, 24*, 1650–1659.

Ko, S. J., Ford, J. D., Kassam-Adams, N., Berkowitz, S. J., Wilson, C., & Wong, M. (2008). Creating trauma-informed systems: Child welfare, education, first responders, health care, juvenile justice. *Professional Psychiatry, 39*(4), 396–404.

Overstreet, S., & Chafouleas, S. M. (2016). Trauma-informed schools: Introduction to the special issue. *School Mental Health, 8*, 1–6.

Perry, D. L., & Daniels, M. L. (2016). Implementing trauma-informed practices in the school setting: A pilot study. *School Mental Health, 8*, 177–188.

Phifer, L. W., & Hull, R. (2016). Helping students heal: Observations of trauma-informed practices in schools. *School Mental Health, 8*, 201–205.

Shamblin, S., Graham, D., & Bianco, J. A. (2016). Creating trauma-informed schools for rural Appalachia: The Partnerships Program for enhancing resiliency, confidence, and workforce development in early childhood education. *School Mental Health, 8,* 189–200.

Substance Abuse and Mental Health Services Administration. (2014). *SAMHSA's concept of trauma and guidance for a trauma-informed approach.* Retrieved from https://store.samhsa.gov/shin/content/SMA14-4884/SMA14-4884.pdf

Sugai, G., & Horner, R. H. (2009). Responsiveness-to-intervention and school-wide positive behavior supports: Integration of multitiered system approaches. *Exceptionality: A Special Education Journal, 17*(4), 223–237.

Walkley, M., & Cox, T. L. (2013). Building trauma-informed schools and communities. *Children & Schools, 35*(2), 123–126.

8

Evaluating Trauma-Informed School Social Work

This final chapter provides a program evaluation strategy for trauma-informed school social workers to utilize in determining the success of their programs and to adapt programs as needed based on outcomes. The aim is to build and expand the literature on empirically-supported and evidence-based practices in school setting.

Most school administrators and teachers agree that they want to create learning environments that are safe for all children. However, recognizing that some dynamics within the school environment can feel unsafe to children who have experienced trauma, and changing them, is another matter. Uniform standards for creating trauma-informed environments and metrics for evaluating their success are currently lacking in the fields of education and social work (Baker et al., 2016). In fact, consistent definitions of trauma-informed care and its essential components are still developing in the scholarly literature (Hanson & Lang, 2016). We are beginning to see some guidance from federal agencies (SAMHSA, 2014) and from some newly created trauma-informed schools and districts in the United States (Overstreet & Chafouleas, 2016).

As we reviewed in previous chapters, children who experienced abuse, neglect, and other forms of trauma often have difficulties learning in school and can be difficult to manage in the classroom because of acting-out behaviors. Research showing improvements in school performance when managing the effects of trauma is encouraging (Rolfsnes & Isdoe, 2011). As more schools understand the connection between truancy, discipline referrals, suspensions, expulsions, dropouts, low academic performance, mental health issues, and trauma, the value of developing trauma-informed learning environments becomes more apparent. School social workers can lead the change process by using our knowledge, skills, and experience about why trauma-informed school practices are needed. Creating a plan for evaluating the changes will be an important step in this process. Each setting must be able to answer the question, "How will we know if we succeed?" In other words, what are the measures that indicate that a school is truly trauma-informed? By mapping out both the processes and outcomes that require change, school social workers are able to measure the impact of trauma-informed work (Chafouleas et al., 2016). This chapter helps you figure out how to approach this task.

Evaluating Assumptions

Every school is different and faces unique challenges to creating a trauma-informed environment. The first step is to understand the assumptions behind *why* schools need to be trauma-informed. In some instances, these changes come about as a response to federal policies such as the Every Student Succeeds Act (P.L. 114-95) or to local funding opportunities. In some instances, the school social worker is leading the effort. Regardless of the impetus for this change, the assumptions behind why it is needed should be sound. The ten principles of trauma-informed services outlined in Chapter 5 are summarized in four general assumptions that must be upheld in any system that chooses to undergo this change (SAMHSA, 2014). For schools in particular, this means that they must assume that:

1. Childhood trauma is pervasive in the general population and has profound lasting impacts. There are a large number of children in schools who experience the effects of current or past trauma that can interfere with being successful in school, and they need trauma-informed school services in order to be successful.
2. Professionals and paraprofessionals in schools can become educated about the signs of exposure to adverse childhood experiences and therefore identify those students who need support.
3. Responses to learning and/or behavioral problems in schoolchildren can be adapted to create responses that are evidence-based and trauma-informed.

4. Preventing retraumatization of children in the school setting, however unintentional, must become a guiding principle for all those who work with schoolchildren.

Evaluating Readiness for Change: Barriers and Attitudes

Getting commitment from leadership, administration, faculty, and staff is essential for permanent change (Nadeem & Ringle, 2016). Even with a nationwide focus on the connection between childhood trauma and educational difficulties (McIntyre et al., 2016), many school systems struggle to adapt trauma-informed systems. In some cases, it feels like an ocean liner trying to take a sharp left turn. There are many different parts to this change and many areas where efforts can go awry. Adequate teacher training and buy-in are essential for widespread implementation (Baweja et al., 2016) of programs in schools and classrooms. Assessing negative attitudes toward trauma-informed care helps determine where the biggest barriers lie and can be done using the Attitudes Related to Trauma-Informed Care (ARTIC) scale (Baker et al., 2016). This scale helps school social workers determine where the attitudinal barriers to change lie, serves as an intervention to understand where more training is needed, and assesses whether trauma-informed efforts are eroding.

A good place to start is to assess readiness for creating a trauma-informed environment. The Agency Self-Assessment is a tool that helps school social workers identify the best path to organizational change, evaluate the implementation, and monitor the efforts on a long-term basis (Harris & Fallot, 2001). This self-assessment process can be led by school social workers to explore ways to support staff development, adapt existing relevant policies, and ultimately create a safe environment for children and professionals in school settings. Frequently used in child welfare settings, the Trauma System Readiness Tool (Chadwick Trauma-Informed Systems Project, 2013) is applicable in school settings. It is used to engage administrators, staff, and front-line workers to determine whether the system is prepared to become trauma-informed.

Creating a realistic timeline for implementation and evaluation is also crucial. Putting in the necessary time to change attitudes and lay the necessary foundation of knowledge and skills on the front end is directly connected to success in the long-term (Perry & Daniels, 2016). Systems change is slow, and therefore efforts to engage in a paradigm shift requires patience and persistence.

Evaluating Training: Knowledge and Skills

For most systems seeking change, one of the first steps is to provide training so that staff may acquire the necessary skills to move toward the desired change. However, a systemic evaluation of that training is often overlooked. In order to determine whether training has achieved the desired goals, the system must explore what changes occurred as a result of the training and if the intended changes were achieved. Evaluating *knowledge* about trauma and trauma-informed services before and after the training is a good first step (Kenny et al., 2017). This is essential because research shows that most graduate programs that educate and train social workers, psychologists, and other mental health professionals do not provide adequate content on trauma (Cook & Newman, 2014; Council on Social Work Education, 2012). This has a very negative impact on children in schools whose behavior is misunderstood and on workers who lack the basic competencies to be effective in their work (Richardson et al., 2012).

As training is being planned and implemented, those responsible for the success of the initiative must keep in mind that those who doubt the need for trauma-informed services in schools are watching closely to see if the effort was worthwhile. Therefore, outcome data are necessary to make sure that this isn't just a "one and done" effort but rather an ongoing system change effort. Kirpatrick and Kirpatrick's (2006) training evaluation model presents some essential elements, including four highly relevant areas for creating trauma-informed schools:

1. *Participant satisfaction with the training*—this is basically a consumer satisfaction component. The evaluation should include questions about the schedule, the presenter, the facility, breaks, food, and so forth. Was the room too cold? Was the seating comfortable? Was the room setup conducive to learning? Would the participants recommend the training to others? If members of a school community are resistant to the initiative, a well-run training program is an essential first step.

2. *Changes to knowledge, skills, and attitudes*—this component of the evaluation addresses what participants learned that they didn't already know. Pretraining and posttraining questions give you some of these data, as can follow-up evaluations six months and one year after the training. These questions should be tied to the learning objectives and

goals for the training. What do you want the participants to know as a result of the training? How will you know that they know it? What activities are part of the training that help participants translate knowledge to skills? How does what trainees learned change how they view children and adolescents who have experienced trauma? By administering a tool, like the Attitudes Related to Trauma-Informed Care assessment (Baker et al., 2016), you measure pretraining and posttraining changes.

3. *Changes to professional behaviors implemented after the training*—for this component, you will need to determine what behavioral changes you want to see in the participants and then create or find a measure for it. This could be as simple as the use of a trauma checklist in assessments or as complex as the adaptation of Trauma-Focused Cognitive Behavioral Therapy (TF-CBT) for group work with adolescents in high schools. What makes this element difficult to achieve is that the data have to be collected at later points in time. Conducting an evaluation of staff behaviors six months or one year after a training is complicated, but it is essential to determine whether the training affected behavior (Kramer et al., 2013).

4. *Cost–benefit analysis of the training's impact*—established by maximizing the number of participants in a training program and keeping training costs low by working with a local mental health professional well-versed in trauma-informed care or by having someone on staff attend a "train the trainer" program and then be the in-house expert for the initiative. Essentially, training must achieve the desired outcome and results while being cost-effective and sustainable.

By building evaluation into the planning process, school social workers can ensure that the skills necessary for trauma-informed services are covered in the training and that the staff are evaluated on their knowledge of the skills and how they implement those skills over time. Research shows that teacher training and education have historically lacked the inclusion of knowledge about trauma and the skills necessary to manage traumatized children in the classroom; therefore, providing trauma training for educators and social workers is essential to the success of trauma-informed schools (Phifer & Hull, 2016).

Evaluating Screening and Services

Screening children and adolescents for trauma and referring to services in school settings is a crucial part of trauma-informed care. Taking an inventory of the assessment and screening tools used in the school is a good place to start. How are children with trauma histories identified? What services are they referred to within and outside the school? Adopting valid and reliable tools to include in an assessment helps school social workers identify those children and adolescents who are vulnerable. Finding tools that are reliable, valid, and not too time-consuming to administer and score can be difficult. Briere and colleagues have developed a number of Trauma Symptom Checklists for children (ages 8–16) and young children (ages 3–12). Both have good psychometric properties for identifying children with distressing traumatic experiences (Strand et al., 2005) and must be purchased for use. The Child Trauma Questionnaire and the Traumatic Events Screening Inventory are also good measures for determining which children may be in need of services. These are open source measures and do not carry a fee for use. See Strand et al. (2005) for a more exhaustive list.

Through utilization of valid and reliable measures for trauma, school social workers can also measure the impact of their services. By administering an assessment tool before and after services, preintervention and postintervention data are collected that provide some indication of the effectiveness of social work services in the school setting. These services need to be directly related to trauma symptoms, appropriate for the ages of the children and adolescents, and evidence-based, such as TF-CBT (Holmes et al., 2015). Answering questions regarding the impact of trauma-informed services on behavioral problems and trauma-related symptoms is possible when you have these data (Dorado et al., 2016).

Evaluating Program Outcomes

A Logic Model provides a visual conceptualization for program design, planned change, and expected outcomes. It begins with a description of the context or climate in which a program will be instituted along with underlying assumptions about the problem and external factors that support or thwart the program. The model goes on to identify the inputs (needed resources and infrastructure), the outputs (activities/interventions and participation/

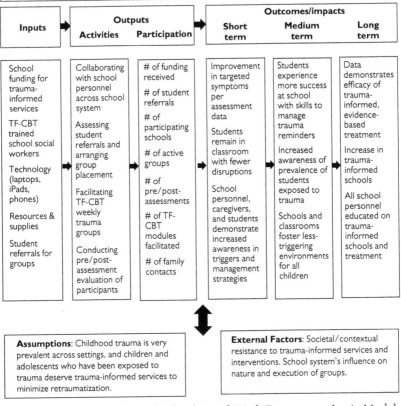

Context: An urban school system whose school social work department provides trauma groups to elementary, middle, and high school students to promote understanding of how trauma affects the body and brain, improve externalizing and internalizing behaviors, and minimize and manage triggers for children and adolescents exposed to trauma.

Inputs	Outputs		Outcomes/impacts		
	Activities	Participation	Short term	Medium term	Long term
School funding for trauma-informed services TF-CBT trained school social workers Technology (laptops, iPads, phones) Resources & supplies Student referrals for groups	Collaborating with school personnel across school system Assessing student referrals and arranging group placement Facilitating TF-CBT weekly trauma groups Conducting pre/post-assessment evaluation of participants	# of funding received # of student referrals # of participating schools # of active groups # of pre/post-assessments # of TF-CBT modules facilitated # of family contacts	Improvement in targeted symptoms per assessment data Students remain in classroom with fewer disruptions School personnel, caregivers, and students demonstrate increased awareness in triggers and management strategies	Students experience more success at school with skills to manage trauma reminders Increased awareness of prevalence of students exposed to trauma Schools and classrooms foster less-triggering environments for all children	Data demonstrates efficacy of trauma-informed, evidence-based treatment Increase in trauma-informed schools All school personnel educated on trauma-informed schools and treatment

Assumptions: Childhood trauma is very prevalent across settings, and children and adolescents who have been exposed to trauma deserve trauma-informed services to minimize retraumatization.

External Factors: Societal/contextual resistance to trauma-informed services and interventions. School system's influence on nature and execution of groups.

Figure 8.1 Trauma-Informed School Social Work Department Logic Model.

data collection), and outcomes or impacts (short-, medium-, and long-term effects of the program) (W. K. Kellogg Foundation, 2006).

The first Logic Model presented in Figure 8.1 is devised for use by school social workers creating groups within a trauma-informed school, while the second Logic Model presented in Figure 8.2 is developed for collaborating with community-based mental health providers to provide groups in a trauma-informed school.

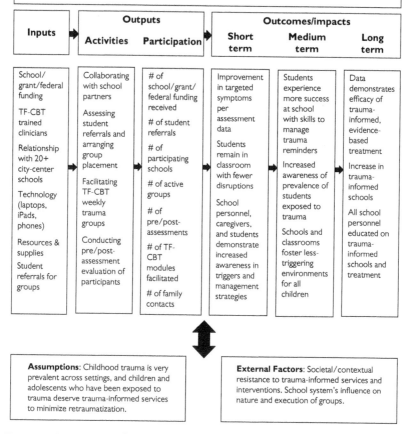

Context: A nonprofit, community agency providing school-based trauma groups in an urban setting seeks to promote understanding of how trauma affects the body and brain, improve externalizing and internalizing behaviors, and minimize and manage triggers for children and adolescents exposed to trauma.

Inputs	Outputs		Outcomes/impacts		
	Activities	Participation	Short term	Medium term	Long term
School/grant/federal funding	Collaborating with school partners	# of school/grant/federal funding received	Improvement in targeted symptoms per assessment data	Students experience more success at school with skills to manage trauma reminders	Data demonstrates efficacy of trauma-informed, evidence-based treatment
TF-CBT trained clinicians	Assessing student referrals and arranging group placement	# of student referrals	Students remain in classroom with fewer disruptions	Increased awareness of prevalence of students exposed to trauma	Increase in trauma-informed schools
Relationship with 20+ city-center schools		# of participating schools			
Technology (laptops, iPads, phones)	Facilitating TF-CBT weekly trauma groups	# of active groups	School personnel, caregivers, and students demonstrate increased awareness in triggers and management strategies	Schools and classrooms foster less-triggering environments for all children	All school personnel educated on trauma-informed schools and treatment
		# of pre/post-assessments			
Resources & supplies	Conducting pre/post-assessment evaluation of participants	# of TF-CBT modules facilitated			
Student referrals for groups		# of family contacts			

Assumptions: Childhood trauma is very prevalent across settings, and children and adolescents who have been exposed to trauma deserve trauma-informed services to minimize retraumatization.

External Factors: Societal/contextual resistance to trauma-informed services and interventions. School system's influence on nature and execution of groups.

Figure 8.2 Trauma-Informed School-Based Community Agency Logic Model.

Resources

Tool Name	Purpose	Web Link
Agency Self-Assessment	Planning system change; target opportunities	traumainformedcareproject.org
Attitudes Related to Trauma-Informed Care (ARTIC)	Measuring attitudes; assessing barriers to change	traumaticstressinstitute.org/artic-scale/
Child Trauma Questionnaire (CTQ)	Screening adolescents age 12+	www.midss.org/sites/default/files/ trauma.pdf
Trauma Informed System Change Instrument	Measuring systems changes that have resulted from trauma-informed care initiatives	Traumainformedoregon.org/ wp-content/uploads/2014/10/ Trauma-Informed-System-Change-Instrument-Organizational-Change-Self-Evaluation.pdf
Trauma Symptom Checklists	Measuring trauma symptoms in children and adolescents ages 3–16	https://www.parinc.com/Products/ Pkey/461(Cost involved in obtaining instruments)
Trauma System Readiness Tool	Measuring knowledge about trauma; addressing service coordination	ctisp.org/trauma-informed-child-welfare-practice-toolkit/
Traumatic Events Screening Inventory for Children (TESI-C)	Assessing child's experiences of traumatic events	https://www.ptsd.va.gov/professional/ assessment/child/tesi.asp

Additional research and scholarship can be found with the following search engines:

Campbell Collaboration: https://campbellcollaboration.org

Center for School Mental Health: http://csmh.umaryland.edu

Cochrane Library: http://www.cochranelibrary.com

School Social Work Association of America: Evidence-Based Practice: https://www.sswaa. org/evidence-based-practice

What Works Clearinghouse: https://ies.ed.gov/ncee/wwc/

References

Baweja, S., DeCarlo Santiago, C., Vona, P., Pears, G., Langley, A., & Kataoka, S. (2015). Improving implementation of a school-based program for traumatized students: Identifying factors that promote teacher support and collaboration. *School Mental Health, 8*(1), 120–131.

Baker, C. N., Brown, S. M., Wilcox, P. D., Overstreet, S., & Arora, P. (2016). Development and psychometric evaluation of the Attitudes Related to Trauma-Informed Care (ARTIC) scale. *School Mental Health, 8*(1), 61–76.

Chadwick Trauma-Informed Systems Project. (2013). *Trauma system readiness tool.* Chadwick Center for Children and Families. San Diego, CA: Author.

Chafouleas, S. M., Johnson, A. H., Overstreet, S., & Santos, N. M. (2016). Toward a blueprint for trauma-informed service delivery in schools. *School Mental Health, 8*(1), 144–162.

Cook, J. M., & Newman, E. (2014). A consensus statement on trauma mental health: The New Haven Competency Conference process and major findings. *Psychological Trauma: Theory, Research, Practice, and Policy, 1*(1), 300–307.

Council on Social Work Education. (2012). *Advanced social work practice in trauma.* Alexandria, VA: Author.

Dorado, J. S., Martinez, M., McArthur, L. E., & Leibovitz, T. (2016). Healthy Environments and Response to Trauma in Schools (HEARTS): A whole-school, multi-level, prevention and intervention program for creating trauma-informed, safe and supportive schools. *School Mental Health, 8*(1), 163–176.

Hanson, R. F., & Lang, J. (2016). A critical look at trauma-informed care among agencies and systems serving maltreated youth and families. *Child Maltreatment, 21*(2), 95–100.

Harris, M., & Fallot, R. (Eds.) (2001). *Using trauma theory to design service systems.* New Directions for Mental Health Services. San Francisco, CA: Jossey-Bass.

Holmes, C., Levy, M., Smith, A., Pinne, S., & Neese, P. (2015). A model for creating a supportive trauma-informed culture for children in preschool settings. *Journal of Child and Family Studies, 24*, 1650–1659.

Kenny, M. C., Vazquez, A., Long, H., & Thompson, D. (2017). Implementation and program evaluation of trauma-informed care training across state child advocacy centers: An exploratory study. *Children and Youth Services Review, 73*, 15–23.

Kirpatrick, D., & Kirpatrick, J. (2006). *Evaluating training programs: The four levels* (3rd ed.). San Francisco, CA: Berrett-Koehler Publishers.

Kramer, T. L., Sigel, B. A., Conners-Burrow, N. A., Savary, P. E., & Tempel, A. (2013). A statewide introduction of trauma-informed care in a child welfare system. *Children and Youth Services Review, 35*, 19–24.

McIntyre, E., Simon, K., Petrovic, L., Chafouleas, S. M., & Overstreet, S. (2016). Toolbox for student trauma: Highlighting the school mental health special issue on trauma-informed schools. *Communiqué, 44*(8), 26–27.

Nadeem, E., & Ringle, V. (2016). De-adoption of an evidence-based trauma intervention in schools: A retrospective report from an urban school district. *School Mental Health, 8*(1), 132–143.

Overstreet, S., & Chafouleas, S. M. (2016). Trauma-informed schools: Introduction to the Special Issue. *School Mental Health, 8*(1), 1–6.

Perry, D. L., & Daniels, M. L. (2016). Implementing trauma-informed practices in school settings: A pilot study. *School Mental Health, 8*(1), 177–188.

Phifer, L. W., & Hull, R. (2016). Helping students heal: Observations of trauma-informed practices in the schools. *School Mental Health, 8*(1), 201–205.

Richardson, M. M., Cotyn, C. L., Henry, J., Black-Pond, C., & Unrau, Y. (2012). Development and evaluation of the Trauma-Informed System Change Instrument: Factorial validity and implications for use. *Child and Adolescent Social Work Journal, 29*, 167–184.

Rolfsnes, E. S., & Isdoe, T. (2011). School-based intervention programs for PTSD symptoms: A review and meta-analysis. *Journal of Traumatic Stress, 24*, 155–165.

Strand, V. C., Sarmiento, T. L., & Pasquale, L. E. (2005). Assessment and screening tools for trauma in children and adolescents: A review. *Trauma, Violence, & Abuse, 6*(1), 55–78.

Substance Abuse and Mental Health Services Administration. (2014). SAMHSA's concept of trauma and guidance for a trauma-informed approach (HHS Publication No, 14-4884). Retrieved from https://store.samhsa.gov/shin/content/SMA14-4884/SMA14-4884.pdf.

W. K. Kellogg Foundation. (2006). Logic model development guide. Retrieved from https://www.wkkf.org/resource-directory/resource/2006/02/wk-kellogg-foundation-logic-model-development-guide

Index

Page numbers followed by *f* indicate figures; page numbers followed by *t* indicate tables; page numbers followed by *b* indicate boxes

modulation, 69. *See also* self-regulation

mood disorders, 15

National Alliance for Grieving Children, 7

National Association of Social Workers (NASW), 20

National Association of Social Workers (NASW) Press, 6–7

National Child Traumatic Stress Network, 36

National Child Traumatic Stress Network (NCTSN), 4–5

National Child Traumatic Stress Network (NCTSN) TF-CBT WEB, 75

National Institute for Trauma and Loss in Children, 7

National Institute of Mental Health (NIMH), 6

National Sexual Violence Resource Center, 65

neurobiology of trauma, 11–14, 73–74

New Haven Trauma Coalition (NHTC), 83

Office for Victims of Crime, 65

Oxford University Press, 7

posttraumatic stress disorder (PTSD), 26–27
  ADHD and, 26–27, 72
  conduct disorder and, 27–28

preschool setting, 81–82

professional development, 83

professional learning communities, 79

Professional Quality of Life, 65

program outcomes, evaluating, 95–96

psychological problems, 12, 15–16

Raines, Jim, 18–19

recovery from trauma
  trauma-informed services identify recovery as primary goal, 60
  trauma-informed services strive to maximize person's choice and control over, 61

regulation. *See* affect regulation; emotional regulation; self-regulation

relational collaboration, trauma-informed services based in a, 61–62

religiosity, 17

resilience
  highlighting, 62–63
  measures of, 18–19
  as moderating influence, 18–19

respect, trauma-informed services create atmosphere respectful of survivors' need for, 62

retraumatization, minimizing the possibility of, 63, 80

RICH (Respect, Information, Connection, and Hope) relationship, 61–62

routines and rituals, caregivers supporting, 69